The Merchant of Venice
Annotation-Friendly Edition

William Shakespeare

This book is also available in large-print, extra large print and dyslexia-friendly editions

Key Themes

friendship/loyalty
love/marriage/romance
} relationships

gender roles
hierarchy
} societal roles

wealth/money } personal gain

prejudice
justice/mercy
revenge
} hatred   ⎯⎯ = religion

firestonebooks.com

general anotations } doesn't fit theme

The Merchant of Venice
Annotation-Friendly Edition

William Shakespeare

2019 Edition

Published by Firestone Books

ISBN-13: 9781796729290

All rights reserved. This publication may not be reproduced or transmitted in any form or by any means, electronic, mechanical, photocopying, recording or otherwise without prior permission from Firestone Books.

firestonebooks.com

You can also find out more by following Firestone Books on Facebook and Twitter

CONTENTS

A Quick Guide to Successful Annotating
William Shakespeare – A Brief Biography
Introduction

THE MERCHANT OF VENICE   11

Glossary of Literary Terms   159
The Merchant of Venice Glossary   162

A Quick Guide to Successful Annotating

- Write down any thoughts you have as you go along
- Highlight key points, either with a highlighter or by underlining
- Note any literary techniques in the margins. (The *Glossary of Literary Terms* at the back of the book should help)
- Define any words you don't understand – it will help you later
- Look for patterns, such as repeating words and phrases
- Pick out key points that show a character's development
- Summarise your thoughts on the blank pages at the end of each act
- Once you've finished reading the play, go back and add to your notes. In particular look at foreshadowing, echoing and motifs

William Shakespeare – A Brief Biography

William Shakespeare was born in Stratford-upon-Avon, the son of John Shakespeare, a successful glove-maker, and Mary Arden, the daughter of a prosperous farmer. His date of birth is unknown but he was baptised, most likely within a few days of his birth, on 26th April 1564.

It is likely that Shakespeare attended the King's New School in Stratford-upon-Avon where he would have received a classical education. He did not attend university, and at the age of eighteen he married Anne Hathaway who was eight years his senior. Six months later, in May 1583, Anne gave birth to a daughter, Susanna. In 1585 Anne also gave birth to twins, Hamnet and Judith.

Between 1585 and 1592 almost nothing is known of Shakespeare's life, the so called "lost years". Many apocryphal tales about this period have been reported including that he fled his hometown for London to escape prosecution for deer poaching, that he started his theatrical career minding the horses of wealthy theatregoers, and that he may have been briefly employed as a schoolmaster in Lancashire.

By 1592 Shakespeare was an established playwright, with several of his plays having been staged in London. It is also the year that fellow playwright, Robert Greene, published his infamous *Groats-Worth of Wit* in which he attacked Shakespeare for trying to match the writing of university educated writers such as Christopher Marlowe and Thomas Nashe.

Shakespeare's plays were only performed by the Lord Chamberlain's Men, a company of actors, in which Shakespeare had a share.

In 1596, Shakespeare's only son, Hamnet, died, and

while in later years Shakespeare's daughters would marry and have four children between them, none of Shakespeare's grandchildren would have children of their own, and so in 1670 with the death of his granddaughter, Elizabeth, his direct line was ended.

In 1599 some members of the Lord Chamberlain's Men built their own theatre on the south bank of the river Thames and named it the Globe. As a shareholder in this theatre, holding up to 3000 spectators, Shakespeare became a wealthy man.

Prior to 1599 Shakespeare had only written two tragedies: *Titus Andronicus* and *Romeo and Juliet*, with his focus being more on comedies, history plays and poems. After 1599 he almost stopped writing history plays and instead switched to writing tragedies, writing many of his finest plays including: *Hamlet, Othello, King Lear* and *Macbeth.*

In 1603 the new king, James I, awarded the Lord Chamberlain's Men a royal patent and the company changed its name to the King's Men.

As well as writing plays, Shakespeare also wrote two long poems and a collection of sonnets. The sonnets describe two love affairs, but who these lovers were – or even if they were real or imagined – remains a mystery.

As Shakespeare was also an actor, it meant that rather than working on his plays in isolation he would have worked closely with other actors. Many of the plots for the plays came from history books, or earlier Italian tales, so it is difficult, if not impossible, to work out what contributions were Shakespeare's. Even when he'd finished a particular play, it was still likely to be re-worked by actors and others – something that is done to this day and keeps his work as fresh and interesting as its ever been.

Though Shakespeare worked as a writer and actor

in London for most of his adult life, his did spend much of his time in Stratford-upon-Avon where, in 1597, he bought New Place as his family home. It's known that Shakespeare was still working as an actor in London in 1608, and that he also retired to Stratford 'some years before his death'.

Shakespeare died on the 23rd of April 1616, around the time of his 52nd birthday. It was said by John Ward, the vicar of Stratford, writing in the mid-1600s that 'Shakespeare, Drayton and Ben Johnson had a merry meeting and, it seems, drank too hard, for Shakespeare died of a fever there contracted.'

Shakespeare was buried at the Holy Trinity Church, the place of his baptism over half a century earlier. The epitaph on his gravestone has a curse against disturbing his resting place:

Good friend, for Jesus' sake forbear,
To dig the dust enclosed here.
Blessed be the man that spares these stones,
And cursed be he that moves my bones.

Fellow dramatist, Ben Johnson, famously and presciently referred to Shakespeare as being 'not of an age, but for all time.' Since his death Shakespeare's reputation has grown, leading him to now be widely regarded as the greatest writer in the English language and the world's greatest dramatist.

Introduction

Shakespeare's *The Merchant of Venice*, though considered a comedy, is as well-known for its dramatic scenes as for its humour.

Written at the end of the sixteenth century between about 1596 and 1598, *The Merchant of Venice,* has its origins in earlier Italian tales. Shakespeare made much use of Italian tales for his works, including: *Romeo and Juliet, Othello* and *Much Ado About Nothing.*

Spoiler alert – if you do not know what happens in *The Merchant of Venice*, you may wish to stop reading the introduction now and return to it after reading the play.

When writing *The Merchant of Venice,* Shakespeare made use of numerous literary sources. A number of elements in this play such as the test of the suitors at Belmont, the merchant's rescue by his friend's wife disguised as a lawyer, and her demand for the betrothal ring as payment are present in *Il Pecorone* by Giovanni Fiorentino, which was published in 1558. The story of the three caskets can be found in *Gesta Romanorum,* a collection of tales most likely compiled around the end of the thirteenth century. Elements of the trial scene are also found in *The Orator* by Alexandre Sylvane, the English translation being first published in 1596.

Love, relationships, money and mercy are themes that run through the play. On the surface it appears that the Christian characters are good, by and large, and place great value on relationships, while the Jewish character, Shylock, is an unpleasant person who places great value on money. Shylock, who is owed a substantial amount of money, request that he is given a literal pound of Antonio's flesh if the debt is not repaid on time. When the debt remains unpaid after the specified date, Shylock refuses to accept twice the amount of the loan, showing he puts more value on the flesh than on money. It also shows him at his unmerciful worst.

With regards the Christian characters, who are in the main portrayed as loving, compassionate and merciful, these ideals break down somewhat when analysed carefully. Portia manages to strip Shylock of his bond and his estate, and forces him to beg for mercy. He is forced to convert to Christianity, he loses his profession as moneylender, and half his goods are confiscated.

The Merchant of Venice is a brilliantly plotted tale, where there's always more to each character than first meets the eye. It is also a play that begs many questions: Was it Antonio's blatant antisemitism that caused Shylock to demand a pound of Antonio's flesh? Is it in fact the Christian characters that have brought out the worst in Shylock? Is the central theme of the play a comparison of Christian mercy versus Jewish vengefulness? Is it possible that Shylock's forced conversion to Christianity was seen by audiences in Shakespeare's time as a happy ending for Shylock as now his soul might be saved? Is it right to see *The Merchant of Venice* as a comedy? Should Shylock be viewed as a tragic figure?

The Merchant of Venice is a fascinating play that has enthralled audiences for centuries and no doubt will continue to be enjoyed for generations to come.

David Lear
Editor – Firestone Books

THE MERCHANT OF VENICE

DRAMATIS PERSONAE

DUKE OF VENICE.

PRINCE OF MOROCCO & PRINCE

OF ARRAGON, Suitors to Portia.

ANTONIO, a Merchant of Venice.

BASSANIO, his Friend.

GRATIANO, SALANIO, & SALARINO: Friends to

Antonio and Bassanio.

LORENZO, in love with Jessica.

SHYLOCK, a rich Jew.

TUBAL, a Jew, his Friend.

LAUNCELOT GOBBO, a Clown, Servant to

Shylock.

OLD GOBBO, Father to Launcelot.

LEONARDO, Servant to Bassanio.

BALTHAZAR & STEPHANO: Servants to Portia.

PORTIA, a rich Heiress.

NERISSA, her Waiting-maid.

JESSICA, Daughter to Shylock.

Magnificoes of Venice, Officers of the Court of Justice, Gaoler, Servants to Portia, and other Attendants.

SCENE.—*Partly at Venice, and partly at Belmont, the seat of Portia, on the Continent.*

ACT I

SCENE I. Venice. A street.

[*Enter ANTONIO, SALARINO, and SALANIO*]

ANTONIO: In sooth, I know not why I am so sad:

It wearies me; you say it wearies you;

But how I caught it, found it, or came by it,

What stuff 'tis made of, whereof it is born,

I am to learn;

And such a want-wit sadness makes of me,

That I have much ado to know myself.

SALARINO: Your mind is tossing on the ocean;

There, where your argosies with portly sail,

Like signiors and rich burghers on the flood,

Or, as it were, the pageants of the sea,

Do overpeer the petty traffickers,

That curtsy to them, do them reverence,

As they fly by them with their woven wings.

SALANIO: Believe me, sir, had I such venture

forth,

The better part of my affections would

Be with my hopes abroad. I should be still

Plucking the grass, to know where sits the wind,

Peering in maps for ports and piers and roads;
And every object that might make me fear
Misfortune to my ventures, out of doubt
Would make me sad.

SALARINO: My wind cooling my broth
Would blow me to an ague, when I thought
What harm a wind too great at sea might do.
I should not see the sandy hour-glass run,
But I should think of shallows and of flats,
And see my wealthy Andrew dock'd in sand,
Vailing her high-top lower than her ribs
To kiss her burial. Should I go to church
And see the holy edifice of stone,
And not bethink me straight of dangerous rocks,
Which touching but my gentle vessel's side,
Would scatter all her spices on the stream,
Enrobe the roaring waters with my silks,
And, in a word, but even now worth this,
And now worth nothing? Shall I have the thought
To think on this, and shall I lack the thought
That such a thing bechanced would make me
sad?
But tell not me; I know, Antonio
Is sad to think upon his merchandise.

ANTONIO: Believe me, no: I thank my fortune

for it,

My ventures are not in one bottom trusted,

Nor to one place; nor is my whole estate

Upon the fortune of this present year: → claims money doesn't cause him sorrow

Therefore my merchandise makes me not sad.

SALARINO: Why, then you are in love.

ANTONIO: Fie, fie! → definite he isn't too defensive?

SALARINO: Not in love neither? Then let us say

you are sad,

Because you are not merry: and 'twere as easy

For you to laugh and leap and say you are

merry,

Because you are not sad. Now, by two-headed

Janus,

Nature hath framed strange fellows in her time:

Some that will evermore peep through their eyes

And laugh like parrots at a bag-piper,

And other of such vinegar aspect

That they'll not show their teeth in way of smile,

Though Nestor swear the jest be laughable.

[*Enter BASSANIO, LORENZO, and GRATIANO*]

SALANIO: Here comes Bassanio, your most

noble kinsman,

Gratiano and Lorenzo. Fare ye well:

We leave you now with better company.

SALARINO: I would have stay'd till I had made you merry,

If worthier friends had not prevented me.

ANTONIO: Your worth is very dear in my regard.

I take it, your own business calls on you

And you embrace the occasion to depart.

SALARINO: Good morrow, my good lords.

BASSANIO: Good signiors both, when shall we laugh? say, when?

You grow exceeding strange: must it be so?

SALARINO: We'll make our leisures to attend on yours.

[*Exeunt Salarino and Salanio*]

LORENZO: My Lord Bassanio, since you have found Antonio,

We two will leave you: but at dinner-time,

I pray you, have in mind where we must meet.

BASSANIO: I will not fail you.

GRATIANO: You look not well, Signior Antonio;

You have too much respect upon the world:

They lose it that do buy it with much care:

Believe me, you are marvellously changed.

ANTONIO: I hold the world but as the world,
Gratiano;
A stage where every man must play a part,
And mine a sad one.

GRATIANO: Let me play the fool:
With mirth and laughter let old wrinkles come,
And let my liver rather heat with wine
Than my heart cool with mortifying groans.
Why should a man, whose blood is warm within,
Sit like his grandsire cut in alabaster?
Sleep when he wakes and creep into the jaundice
By being peevish? I tell thee what, Antonio—
I love thee, and it is my love that speaks—
There are a sort of men whose visages
Do cream and mantle like a standing pond,
And do a wilful stillness entertain,
With purpose to be dress'd in an opinion
Of wisdom, gravity, profound conceit,
As who should say 'I am Sir Oracle,
And when I ope my lips let no dog bark!'
O my Antonio, I do know of these
That therefore only are reputed wise
For saying nothing; when, I am very sure,

If they should speak, would almost damn those ears,

Which, hearing them, would call their brothers fools.

I'll tell thee more of this another time:

But fish not, with this melancholy bait,

For this fool gudgeon, this opinion.

Come, good Lorenzo. Fare ye well awhile:

I'll end my exhortation after dinner.

LORENZO: Well, we will leave you then till dinner-time:

I must be one of these same dumb wise men,

For Gratiano never lets me speak.

GRATIANO: Well, keep me company but two years moe,

Thou shalt not know the sound of thine own tongue.

ANTONIO: Farewell: I'll grow a talker for this gear.

GRATIANO: Thanks, i' faith, for silence is only commendable

In a neat's tongue dried and a maid not vendible.

[*Exeunt GRATIANO and LORENZO*]

ANTONIO: Is that any thing now?

BASSANIO: Gratiano speaks an infinite deal of nothing, more than any man in all Venice. His reasons are as two grains of wheat hid in two bushels of chaff: you shall seek all day ere you find them, and when you have them, they are not worth the search.

ANTONIO: Well, tell me now what lady is the same

To whom you swore a secret pilgrimage,

That you to-day promised to tell me of?

BASSANIO: 'Tis not unknown to you, Antonio,

How much I have disabled mine estate,

By something showing a more swelling port

Than my faint means would grant continuance:

Nor do I now make moan to be abridged

From such a noble rate; but my chief care

Is to come fairly off from the great debts

Wherein my time something too prodigal

Hath left me gaged. To you, Antonio,

I owe the most, in money and in love,

And from your love I have a warranty

To unburden all my plots and purposes

How to get clear of all the debts I owe.

ANTONIO: I pray you, good Bassanio, let me

know it;

And if it stand, as you yourself still do,

Within the eye of honour, be assured,

money, person and protection are Bassanio's loyalty

everything that is his is Bassanio's also

My purse, my person, my extremest means,

Lie all unlock'd to your occasions.

usually protected

BASSANIO: In my school-days, when I had lost one shaft,

I shot his fellow of the self-same flight

The self-same way with more advised watch,

To find the other forth, and by adventuring both

I oft found both: I urge this childhood proof,

Because what follows is pure innocence.

already squandered Antonio's money before, untrustworthy, greedy, foolish

I owe you much, and, like a wilful youth,

That which I owe is lost; but if you please

if he wishes to lend money again to him

To shoot another arrow that self way

which he has already. I don't doubt

Which you did shoot the first, I do not doubt,

he'll make sure to return both amounts

As I will watch the aim, or to find both

or bring back the 2nd amount again

Or bring your latter hazard back again

appreciate his mercy for the first

And thankfully rest debtor for the first.

ANTONIO: You know me well, and herein spend but time

To wind about my love with circumstance;

And out of doubt you do me now more wrong

In making question of my uttermost

Than if you had made waste of all I have:

Then do but say to me what I should do·

That in your knowledge may by me be done,

And I am prest unto it: therefore, speak.

BASSANIO: In Belmont is a lady richly left; → mentions money first

And she is fair, and, fairer than that word, → then beauty

Of wondrous virtues: sometimes from her eyes

I did receive fair speechless messages: → already believes he has a chance

Her name is Portia, nothing undervalued

To Cato's daughter, Brutus' Portia:

Nor is the wide world ignorant of her worth,

For the four winds blow in from every coast → desired by many

Renowned suitors, and her sunny locks → innocent

Hang on her temples like a golden fleece; → greek mythology

Which makes her seat of Belmont Colchos'

strand, → he searched for golden fleece

And many Jasons come in quest of her. → views her as a prize

→ persessive, trying to persudde

O my Antonio, had I but the means → can't do this himself

To hold a rival place with one of them,

I have a mind presages me such thrift,

That I should questionless be fortunate!

ANTONIO: Thou know'st that all my fortunes are

at sea;

Neither have I money nor commodity

To raise a present sum: therefore go forth;

Try what my credit can in Venice do:

That shall be rack'd, even to the uttermost,

To furnish thee to Belmont, to fair Portia.

Go, presently inquire, and so will I,

Where money is, and I no question make

To have it of my trust or for my sake.   [*Exeunt*]

SCENE II: Belmont. A room in PORTIA'S house.

[*Enter PORTIA and NERISSA*]

PORTIA: By my troth, Nerissa, my little body is aweary of this great world.

something bothering her too

NERISSA: You would be, sweet madam, if your miseries were in the same abundance as your good fortunes are: and yet, for aught I see, they are as sick that surfeit with too much as they that starve with nothing. It is no mean happiness therefore, to be seated in the mean: superfluity comes sooner by white hairs, but competency lives longer.

She's rich so can't be sad

PORTIA: Good sentences and well pronounced.

NERISSA: They would be better, if well followed.

→ feels she never listens

PORTIA: If to do were as easy as to know what were good to do, chapels had been churches and poor men's cottages princes' palaces. It is a good divine that follows his own instructions: I can easier teach twenty what were good to be done, than be one of the twenty to follow mine own teaching. The brain may devise laws for the blood, but a hot temper leaps o'er a cold decree: *(situation changes practice)* such a hare is madness the youth, to skip o'er the meshes of good counsel the cripple. But this reasoning is not in the fashion to choose me a *(understands the irony)* husband. O me, the word 'choose!' I may neither *(she knows she has no choice)* choose whom I would nor refuse whom I dislike; so is the will of a living daughter curbed by the *(dead men have more rights than living women)* will of a dead father. Is it not hard, Nerissa, that I cannot choose one nor refuse none?

NERISSA: Your father was ever virtuous; and holy men at their death have good inspirations: *(feels it fair)* therefore the lottery, that he hath devised in these three chests of gold, silver and lead, *(he wants to make sure he's right)* whereof who chooses his meaning chooses you, will, no doubt, never be chosen by any rightly but one who shall rightly love. But what warmth is there in your affection towards any of these princely suitors that are already come?

PORTIA: I pray thee, over-name them; and as thou namest them, I will describe them; and, according to my description, level at my affection.

NERISSA: First, there is the Neapolitan prince.

PORTIA: Ay, that's a colt indeed, for he doth nothing but talk of his horse; and he makes it a great appropriation to his own good parts, that he can shoe him himself. I am much afeard my lady his mother played false with a smith.

NERISSA: Then there is the County Palatine.

PORTIA: He doth nothing but frown, as who should say 'If you will not have me, choose:' he hears merry tales and smiles not: I fear he will prove the weeping philosopher when he grows old, being so full of unmannerly sadness in his youth. I had rather be married to a death's-head with a bone in his mouth than to either of these. God defend me from these two!

NERISSA: How say you by the French lord, Monsieur Le Bon?

PORTIA: God made him, and therefore let him pass for a man. In truth, I know it is a sin to be a mocker: but, he! why, he hath a horse better than the Neapolitan's, a better bad habit of frowning than the Count Palatine; he is every man in no man; if a throstle sing, he falls straight a capering: he will fence with his own shadow: if I should marry him, I should marry twenty husbands. If he would despise me I would forgive him, for if he love me to madness, I shall never requite him.

NERISSA: What say you, then, to Falconbridge, the young baron of England?

PORTIA: You know I say nothing to him, for he understands not me, nor I him: he hath neither Latin, French, nor Italian, and you will come into the court and swear that I have a poor pennyworth in the English. He is a proper man's picture, but, alas, who can converse with a dumb-show? How oddly he is suited! I think he bought his doublet in Italy, his round hose in France, his bonnet in Germany and his behaviour every where.

NERISSA: What think you of the Scottish lord, his neighbour?

PORTIA: That he hath a neighbourly charity in

him, for he borrowed a box of the ear of the Englishman and swore he would pay him again when he was able: I think the Frenchman became his surety and sealed under for another.

NERISSA: How like you the young German, the Duke of Saxony's nephew?

PORTIA: Very vilely in the morning, when he is sober, and most vilely in the afternoon, when he is drunk: when he is best, he is a little worse than a man, and when he is worst, he is little better than a beast: and the worst fall that ever fell, I hope I shall make shift to go without him.

knows what she does & does not want

NERISSA: If he should offer to choose, and choose the right casket, you should refuse to perform your father's will, if you should refuse to accept him.

suggest breaking the rules

PORTIA: Therefore, for fear of the worst, I pray thee, set a deep glass of rhenish wine on the contrary casket, for if the devil be within and that temptation without, I know he will choose it. I will do any thing, Nerissa, ere I'll be married to a sponge. → humour

irony & humour

as much as she complains still she follows her father's rules

NERISSA: You need not fear, lady, the having any of these lords: they have acquainted me with their determinations; which is, indeed, to return to their home and to trouble you with no more suit, unless you may be won by some other sort than your father's imposition depending on the caskets.

PORTIA: If I live to be as old as Sibylla, I will die as chaste as Diana, unless I be obtained by the manner of my father's will. I am glad this parcel of wooers are so reasonable, for there is not one among them but I dote on his very absence, and I pray God grant them a fair departure.

NERISSA: Do you not remember, lady, in your father's time, a Venetian, a scholar and a soldier, that came hither in company of the Marquis of Montferrat?

PORTIA: Yes, yes, it was Bassanio; as I think, he was so called.

NERISSA: True, madam: he, of all the men that ever my foolish eyes looked upon, was the best deserving a fair lady. ⟶ *believe him most suited*

PORTIA: I remember him well, and I remember him worthy of thy praise. ⟶ *Portia agrees*

[*Enter a Serving-man*]

How now! what news?

Servant: The four strangers seek for you, madam, to take their leave: and there is a forerunner come from a fifth, the Prince of Morocco, who brings word the prince his master will be here to-night.

PORTIA: If I could bid the fifth welcome with so good a heart as I can bid the other four farewell, I should be glad of his approach: if he have the condition of a saint and the complexion of a devil, I had rather he should shrive me than wive me. Come, Nerissa. Sirrah, go before. Whiles we shut the gates upon one wooer, another knocks at the door.

[*Exeunt*]

desired

SCENE III. Venice. A public place.

[*Enter BASSANIO and SHYLOCK*]

SHYLOCK: Three thousand ducats; well.

BASSANIO: Ay, sir, for three months.

SHYLOCK: For three months; well.

BASSANIO: For the which, as I told you, Antonio shall be bound.

SHYLOCK: Antonio shall become bound; well.

BASSANIO: May you stead me? will you pleasure me? shall I know your answer?

SHYLOCK: Three thousand ducats for three months and Antonio bound.

BASSANIO: Your answer to that.

SHYLOCK: Antonio is a good man. —→ *liking control*

BASSANIO: Have you heard any imputation to the contrary?—→ *stands up for him*

SHYLOCK: Oh, no, no, no, no: my meaning in saying he is a good man is to have you |—→ *knows he'll stand by his bond* understand me that he is sufficient. Yet his —→ *quite a mud compliment almost mocking, ravishing in the patter* means are in supposition: he hath an argosy bound to Tripolis, another to the Indies; I understand moreover, upon the Rialto, he hath a third at Mexico, a fourth for England, and other ventures he hath, squandered abroad. But ships are but boards, sailors but men: there be land-rats and water-rats, water-thieves and land-thieves, I mean pirates, and then there is the peril of waters, winds and rocks. The man is, notwithstanding, sufficient. Three thousand ducats; I think I may take his bond. |—→ *agrees*

BASSANIO: Be assured you may.

SHYLOCK: I will be assured I may; and, that I

may be assured, I will bethink me. May I speak with Antonio?

[annotation: initially seems a normal present offer]

[margin note: deeper meaning]

BASSANIO: If it please you to dine with us.

SHYLOCK: Yes, to smell pork; to eat of the habitation which your prophet the Nazarite conjured the devil into. I will buy with you, sell with you, talk with you, walk with you, and so following, but I will not eat with you, drink with you, nor pray with you. What news on the Rialto? Who is he comes here?

[margin note: will not partake in their sacred rituals with them]

[*Enter ANTONIO*]

BASSANIO: This is Signior Antonio.

SHYLOCK: [Aside] How like a fawning publican he looks!

[annotation: thoughts]

I hate him for he is a Christian,

But more for that in low simplicity

He lends out money gratis and brings down

The rate of usance here with us in Venice.

[margin note: prejudice however runs deeper than just his religion]

If I can catch him once upon the hip,

I will feed fat the ancient grudge I bear him.

[annotation: greed (Antisemetic prejudice)]

He hates our sacred nation, and he rails,

Even there where merchants most do congregate,

On me, my bargains and my well-won thrift,

[margin note: looking for an opotunity / foreshadowing]

[margin note: has reason - viewed differently by audiences]

32

other worldly
→ witches
Satanic

Which he calls interest. Cursed be my tribe,

→ classic christian attribute

If I forgive him!

→ not worthy of an apology

BASSANIO: Shylock, do you hear?

SHYLOCK: I am debating of my present store,

And, by the near guess of my memory,

I cannot instantly raise up the gross

Of full three thousand ducats. What of that?

Tubal, a wealthy Hebrew of my tribe,

Will furnish me. But soft! how many months

Do you desire?

[*To ANTONIO*]

Rest you fair, good signior;

Your worship was the last man in our mouths.

ANTONIO: Shylock, although I neither lend nor

borrow

By taking nor by giving of excess,

Yet, to supply the ripe wants of my friend,

I'll break a custom. Is he yet possess'd

How much ye would?

SHYLOCK: Ay, ay, three thousand ducats.

ANTONIO: And for three months.

SHYLOCK: I had forgot; three months; you told

me so.

Well then, your bond; and let me see; but hear

you;

Methought you said you neither lend nor borrow
Upon advantage.

ANTONIO: I do never use it.

SHYLOCK: When Jacob grazed his uncle
Laban's sheep–

This Jacob from our holy Abram was,

As his wise mother wrought in his behalf,

The third possessor; ay, he was the third–

ANTONIO: And what of him? did he take
interest?

SHYLOCK: No, not take interest, not, as you
would say,

Directly interest: mark what Jacob did.

When Laban and himself were compromised

That all the eanlings which were streak'd and
pied

Should fall as Jacob's hire, the ewes, being rank,

In the end of autumn turned to the rams,

And, when the work of generation was

Between these woolly breeders in the act,

The skilful shepherd peel'd me certain wands,

And, in the doing of the deed of kind,

He stuck them up before the fulsome ewes,

Who then conceiving did in eaning time

Fall parti-colour'd lambs, and those were

Jacob's.

This was a way to thrive, and he was blest:

And thrift is blessing, if men steal it not.

ANTONIO: This was a venture, sir, that Jacob

served for;

A thing not in his power to bring to pass,

But sway'd and fashion'd by the hand of heaven.

→ God decided it

Was this inserted to make interest good?

Or is your gold and silver ewes and rams?

SHYLOCK: I cannot tell; I make it breed as fast:

But note me, signior.

ANTONIO: Mark you this, Bassanio,

The devil can cite Scripture for his purpose.

An evil soul producing holy witness

Is like a villain with a smiling cheek,

A goodly apple rotten at the heart:

feels Shylock is taking advantage of the Bible denounces what he says

O, what a goodly outside falsehood hath!

SHYLOCK: Three thousand ducats; 'tis a good

round sum.

Three months from twelve; then, let me see; the

rate–

ANTONIO: Well, Shylock, shall we be beholding

to you?

SHYLOCK: Signior Antonio, many a time and oft
In the Rialto you have rated me
About my moneys and my usances:
Still have I borne it with a patient shrug,
For sufferance is the badge of all our tribe.

antisematicism ← You call me misbeliever, cut-throat dog,
And spit upon my Jewish gaberdine,
And all for use of that which is mine own.
Well then, it now appears you need my help:
Go to, then; you come to me, and you say
'Shylock, we would have moneys:' you say so;
You, that did void your rheum upon my beard
And foot me as you spurn a stranger cur
Over your threshold: moneys is your suit
What should I say to you? Should I not say
'Hath a dog money? is it possible
A cur can lend three thousand ducats?' Or

can't believe he's now expected to be kind ← Shall I bend low and in a bondman's key,
With bated breath and whispering humbleness,
Say this;
'Fair sir, you spit on me on Wednesday last;
You spurn'd me such a day; another time
You call'd me dog; and for these courtesies

I'll lend you thus much moneys'? → confused as to the rules here

ANTONIO: I am as like to call thee so again, → admits he prejudice

To spit on thee again, to spurn thee too.

If thou wilt lend this money, lend it not

As to thy friends; for when did friendship take

A breed for barren metal of his friend?

But lend it rather to thine enemy,

Who, if he break, thou mayst with better face

Exact the penalty. }→ reasoning explaining why it's better

SHYLOCK: Why, look you, how you storm!

I would be friends with you and have your love,

Forget the shames that you have stain'd me with, → still in disbelief

Supply your present wants and take no doit

Of usance for my moneys, and you'll not hear

me:

This is kind I offer.

BASSANIO: This were kindness.

SHYLOCK: This kindness will I show.

Go with me to a notary, seal me there

Your single bond; and, in a merry sport,

If you repay me not on such a day,

In such a place, such sum or sums as are → agrees with & follow antonio's reasoning

Express'd in the condition, let the forfeit

Be nominated for an equal pound

strange
request
living up to what
he said

Of your fair flesh, to be cut off and taken

In what part of your body pleaseth me.

ANTONIO: Content, i' faith: I'll seal to such a bond

→ agrees without thought

And say there is much kindness in the Jew.

BASSANIO: You shall not seal to such a bond for me:

doesn't want
Antonio to take
the risk for him

I'll rather dwell in my necessity.

ANTONIO: Why, fear not, man; I will not forfeit it:

Within these two months, that's a month before

This bond expires, I do expect return

Of thrice three times the value of this bond.

SHYLOCK: O father Abram, what these Christians are,

disagrees
with their
beliefs

Whose own hard dealings teaches them suspect

The thoughts of others! Pray you, tell me this;

If he should break his day, what should I gain

By the exaction of the forfeiture?

doesn't feel
it's enough

A pound of man's flesh taken from a man

Is not so estimable, profitable neither,

As flesh of muttons, beefs, or goats. I say,

To buy his favour, I extend this friendship:

If he will take it, so; if not, adieu;

And, for my love, I pray you wrong me not.

→ wants it to go
in his favour

38

ANTONIO: Yes Shylock, I will seal unto this → *agrees again*
bond.

SHYLOCK: Then meet me forthwith at the
notary's; → *official sealed off document*
Give him direction for this merry bond,

And I will go and purse the ducats straight,

See to my house, left in the fearful guard

Of an unthrifty knave, and presently

I will be with you.

ANTONIO: Hie thee, gentle Jew. → *compliment?*
[*Exit Shylock*]

The Hebrew will turn Christian: he grows kind.

BASSANIO: I like not fair terms and a villain's
mind.

ANTONIO: Come on: in this there can be no
dismay;

My ships come home a month before the day.

[*Exeunt*]

My Notes

ACT II

SCENE I. Belmont. A room in PORTIA'S house.

[*Flourish of cornets. Enter the PRINCE OF MOROCCO and his followers; PORTIA, NERISSA, and others of her train*]

MOROCCO: Mislike me not for my complexion, → implications that she's racist

The shadow'd livery of the burnish'd sun,

To whom I am a neighbour and near bred.

Bring me the fairest creature northward born,

Where Phoebus' fire scarce thaws the icicles,

And let us make incision for your love, → links to Shylocks famous speech

To prove whose blood is reddest, his or mine. → no difference

I tell thee, lady, this aspect of mine

Hath fear'd the valiant: by my love I swear

The best-regarded virgins of our clime

Have loved it too: I would not change this hue,

Except to steal your thoughts, my gentle queen.

PORTIA: In terms of choice I am not solely led

By nice direction of a maiden's eyes;

Besides, the lottery of my destiny

Bars me the right of voluntary choosing:

But if my father had not scanted me

And hedged me by his wit, to yield myself

His wife who wins me by that means I told you,

Yourself, renowned prince, then stood as fair

As any comer I have look'd on yet

For my affection.

MOROCCO: Even for that I thank you:

Therefore, I pray you, lead me to the caskets

To try my fortune. By this scimitar

That slew the Sophy and a Persian prince

That won three fields of Sultan Solyman,

I would outstare the sternest eyes that look,

Outbrave the heart most daring on the earth,

Pluck the young sucking cubs from the she-bear,

Yea, mock the lion when he roars for prey,

To win thee, lady. But, alas the while!

If Hercules and Lichas play at dice

Which is the better man, the greater throw

May turn by fortune from the weaker hand:

So is Alcides beaten by his page;

And so may I, blind fortune leading me,

Miss that which one unworthier may attain,

And die with grieving.

PORTIA: You must take your chance,

And either not attempt to choose at all

Or swear before you choose, if you choose wrong

Never to speak to lady afterward

In way of marriage: therefore be advised.

MOROCCO: Nor will not. Come, bring me unto my chance.

PORTIA: First, forward to the temple: after dinner

Your hazard shall be made.

MOROCCO: Good fortune then!

To make me blest or cursed'st among men.

[*Cornets, and exeunt*]

SCENE II. Venice. A street.

[*Enter LAUNCELOT GOBBO*]

LAUNCELOT: Certainly my conscience will serve me to run from this Jew my master. The fiend is at mine elbow and tempts me saying to me 'Gobbo, Launcelot Gobbo, good Launcelot,' or 'good Gobbo,' or good Launcelot Gobbo, use your legs, take the start, run away. My conscience says 'No; take heed,' honest

Launcelot; take heed, honest Gobbo, or, as aforesaid, 'honest Launcelot Gobbo; do not run; scorn running with thy heels.' Well, the most courageous fiend bids me pack: 'Via!' says the fiend; 'away!' says the fiend; 'for the heavens, rouse up a brave mind,' says the fiend, 'and run.' Well, my conscience, hanging about the neck of my heart, says very wisely to me 'My honest friend Launcelot, being an honest man's son,' or rather an honest woman's son; for, indeed, my father did something smack, something grow to, he had a kind of taste; well, my conscience says 'Launcelot, budge not.' 'Budge,' says the fiend. 'Budge not,' says my conscience. 'Conscience,' say I, 'you counsel well;' ' Fiend,' say I, 'you counsel well:' to be ruled by my conscience, I should stay with the Jew my master, who, God bless the mark, is a kind of devil; and, to run away from the Jew, I should be ruled by the fiend, who, saving your reverence, is the devil himself. Certainly the Jew is the very devil incarnal; and, in my conscience, my conscience is but a kind of hard conscience, to offer to counsel me to stay with the Jew. The fiend gives the more friendly counsel: I will run, fiend; my heels are at your command; I will run.

[*Enter Old GOBBO, with a basket*]

GOBBO: Master young man, you, I pray you, which is the way to master Jew's?

LAUNCELOT: [Aside] O heavens, this is my true-begotten father! who, being more than sand-blind, high-gravel blind, knows me not: I will try confusions with him.

GOBBO: Master young gentleman, I pray you, which is the way to master Jew's?

LAUNCELOT: Turn up on your right hand at the next turning, but, at the next turning of all, on your left; marry, at the very next turning, turn of no hand, but turn down indirectly to the Jew's house.

GOBBO: By God's sonties, 'twill be a hard way to hit. Can you tell me whether one Launcelot, that dwells with him, dwell with him or no?

LAUNCELOT: Talk you of young Master Launcelot?

[*Aside*] Mark me now; now will I raise the waters. Talk you

of young Master Launcelot?

GOBBO: No master, sir, but a poor man's son: his father, though I say it, is an honest exceeding poor man and, God be thanked, well to live.

LAUNCELOT: Well, let his father be what a' will, we talk of young Master Launcelot.

GOBBO: Your worship's friend and Launcelot, sir.

LAUNCELOT: But I pray you, ergo, old man, ergo, I beseech you, talk you of young Master Launcelot?

GOBBO: Of Launcelot, an't please your mastership.

LAUNCELOT: Ergo, Master Launcelot. Talk not of Master Launcelot, father; for the young gentleman, according to Fates and Destinies and such odd sayings, the Sisters Three and such branches of learning, is indeed deceased, or, as you would say in plain terms, gone to heaven.

GOBBO: Marry, God forbid! the boy was the very staff of my age, my very prop.

LAUNCELOT: Do I look like a cudgel or a hovel-post, a staff or a prop? Do you know me, father?

GOBBO: Alack the day, I know you not, young gentleman: but, I pray you, tell me, is my boy,

God rest his soul, alive or dead?

LAUNCELOT: Do you not know me, father?

GOBBO: Alack, sir, I am sand-blind; I know you not.

LAUNCELOT: Nay, indeed, if you had your eyes, you might fail of the knowing me: it is a wise father that knows his own child. Well, old man, I will tell you news of your son: give me your blessing: truth will come to light; murder cannot be hid long; a man's son may, but at the length truth will out.

GOBBO: Pray you, sir, stand up: I am sure you are not Launcelot, my boy.

LAUNCELOT: Pray you, let's have no more fooling about it, but give me your blessing: I am Launcelot, your boy that was, your son that is, your child that shall be.

GOBBO: I cannot think you are my son.

LAUNCELOT: I know not what I shall think of that: but I am Launcelot, the Jew's man, and I am sure Margery your wife is my mother.

GOBBO: Her name is Margery, indeed: I'll be sworn, if thou be Launcelot, thou art mine own flesh and blood. Lord worshipped might he be!

what a beard hast thou got! thou hast got more hair on thy chin than Dobbin my fill-horse has on his tail.

LAUNCELOT: It should seem, then, that Dobbin's tail grows backward: I am sure he had more hair of his tail than I have of my face when I last saw him.

GOBBO: Lord, how art thou changed! How dost thou and thy master agree? I have brought him a present. How 'gree you now?

LAUNCELOT: Well, well: but, for mine own part, as I have set up my rest to run away, so I will not rest till I have run some ground. My master's a very Jew: give him a present! give him a halter: I am famished in his service; you may tell every finger I have with my ribs. Father, I am glad you are come: give me your present to one Master Bassanio, who, indeed, gives rare new liveries: if I serve not him, I will run as far as God has any ground. O rare fortune! here comes the man: to him, father; for I am a Jew, if I serve the Jew any longer.

[*Enter BASSANIO, with LEONARDO and other followers*]

BASSANIO: You may do so; but let it be so hasted that supper be ready at the farthest by five of the clock. See these letters delivered; put the liveries to making, and desire Gratiano to come anon to my lodging.

[*Exit a Servant*]

LAUNCELOT: To him, father.

GOBBO: God bless your worship!

BASSANIO: Gramercy! wouldst thou aught with me?

GOBBO: Here's my son, sir, a poor boy, –

LAUNCELOT: Not a poor boy, sir, but the rich Jew's man; that would, sir, as my father shall specify–

GOBBO: He hath a great infection, sir, as one would say, to serve–

LAUNCELOT: Indeed, the short and the long is, I serve the Jew, and have a desire, as my father shall specify–

GOBBO: His master and he, saving your worship's reverence, are scarce cater-cousins–

LAUNCELOT: To be brief, the very truth is that the Jew, having done me wrong, doth cause me, as my father, being, I hope, an old man, shall frutify unto you—

GOBBO: I have here a dish of doves that I would bestow upon your worship, and my suit is—

LAUNCELOT: In very brief, the suit is impertinent to myself, as your worship shall know by this honest old man; and, though I say it, though old man, yet poor man, my father.

BASSANIO: One speak for both. What would you?

LAUNCELOT: Serve you, sir.

GOBBO: That is the very defect of the matter, sir.

BASSANIO: I know thee well; thou hast obtain'd thy suit:
Shylock thy master spoke with me this day,
And hath preferr'd thee, if it be preferment
To leave a rich Jew's service, to become
The follower of so poor a gentleman.

LAUNCELOT: The old proverb is very well parted between my master Shylock and you, sir: you have the grace of God, sir, and he hath enough.

BASSANIO: Thou speak'st it well. Go, father, with thy son.

Take leave of thy old master and inquire

My lodging out. Give him a livery

More guarded than his fellows': see it done.

LAUNCELOT: Father, in. I cannot get a service,

no; I have ne'er a tongue in my head. Well, if any

man in Italy have a fairer table which doth offer

to swear upon a book, I shall have good fortune.

Go to, here's a simple line of life: here's a small

trifle of wives: alas, fifteen wives is nothing!

Eleven widows and nine maids is a simple

coming-in for one man: and then to 'scape

drowning thrice, and to be in peril of my life with

the edge of a feather-bed; here are simple

scapes. Well, if Fortune be a woman, she's a

good wench for this gear. Father, come; I'll take

my leave of the Jew in the twinkling of an eye.

[*Exeunt Launcelot and Old Gobbo*]

BASSANIO: I pray thee, good Leonardo, think

on this:

These things being bought and orderly bestow'd,

Return in haste, for I do feast to-night

My best-esteem'd acquaintance: hie thee, go.

LEONARDO: My best endeavours shall be done

herein.

[*Enter GRATIANO*]

GRATIANO: Where is your master?

LEONARDO: Yonder, sir, he walks.

[*Exit*]

GRATIANO: Signior Bassanio!

BASSANIO: Gratiano!

GRATIANO: I have a suit to you.

BASSANIO: You have obtain'd it.

GRATIANO: You must not deny me: I must go with you to Belmont.

BASSANIO: Why then you must. But hear thee, Gratiano;

Thou art too wild, too rude and bold of voice;

Parts that become thee happily enough

And in such eyes as ours appear not faults;

But where thou art not known, why, there they show

Something too liberal. Pray thee, take pain

To allay with some cold drops of modesty

Thy skipping spirit, lest through thy wild behaviour

I be misconstrued in the place I go to,

And lose my hopes.

GRATIANO: Signior Bassanio, hear me:

If I do not put on a sober habit,

Talk with respect and swear but now and then,

Wear prayer-books in my pocket, look demurely,

Nay more, while grace is saying, hood mine eyes

Thus with my hat, and sigh and say 'amen,'

Use all the observance of civility,

Like one well studied in a sad ostent

To please his grandam, never trust me more.

BASSANIO: Well, we shall see your bearing.

GRATIANO: Nay, but I bar to-night: you shall not gauge me

By what we do to-night.

BASSANIO: No, that were pity:

I would entreat you rather to put on

Your boldest suit of mirth, for we have friends

That purpose merriment. But fare you well:

I have some business.

GRATIANO: And I must to Lorenzo and the rest:

But we will visit you at supper-time.

[*Exeunt*]

SCENE III. The same. A room in SHYLOCK'S house.

[*Enter JESSICA and LAUNCELOT*]

JESSICA: I am sorry thou wilt leave my father so:

Our house is hell, and thou, a merry devil,

Didst rob it of some taste of tediousness.

But fare thee well, there is a ducat for thee:

And, Launcelot, soon at supper shalt thou see

Lorenzo, who is thy new master's guest:

Give him this letter; do it secretly;

And so farewell: I would not have my father

See me in talk with thee.

LAUNCELOT: Adieu! tears exhibit my tongue.

Most beautiful pagan, most sweet Jew! if a

Christian did not play the knave and get thee, I

am much deceived. But, adieu: these foolish

drops do something drown my manly spirit:

adieu.

JESSICA: Farewell, good Launcelot.

[*Exit Launcelot*]

Alack, what heinous sin is it in me

To be ashamed to be my father's child!

But though I am a daughter to his blood,

I am not to his manners. O Lorenzo,

If thou keep promise, I shall end this strife,

Become a Christian and thy loving wife.

[*Exit*]

SCENE IV. The same. A street.

[*Enter GRATIANO, LORENZO, SALARINO, and SALANIO*]

LORENZO: Nay, we will slink away in supper-time,

Disguise us at my lodging and return,

All in an hour.

GRATIANO: We have not made good preparation.

SALARINO: We have not spoke us yet of torchbearers.

SALANIO: 'Tis vile, unless it may be quaintly order'd,

And better in my mind not undertook.

LORENZO: 'Tis now but four o'clock: we have two hours

To furnish us.

[*Enter LAUNCELOT, with a letter*]

Friend Launcelot, what's the news?

LAUNCELOT: An it shall please you to break up this, it shall seem to signify.

LORENZO: I know the hand: in faith, 'tis a fair hand;

And whiter than the paper it writ on

Is the fair hand that writ.

GRATIANO: Love-news, in faith.

LAUNCELOT: By your leave, sir.

LORENZO: Whither goest thou?

LAUNCELOT: Marry, sir, to bid my old master the Jew to sup to-night with my new master the Christian.

LORENZO: Hold here, take this: tell gentle Jessica

I will not fail her; speak it privately.

Go, gentlemen,

[*Exit Launcelot*]

Will you prepare you for this masque tonight?

I am provided of a torch-bearer.

SALANIO: Ay, marry, I'll be gone about it straight.

SALANIO: And so will I.

LORENZO: Meet me and Gratiano

At Gratiano's lodging some hour hence.

SALARINO: 'Tis good we do so.

[*Exeunt SALARINO and SALANIO*]

GRATIANO: Was not that letter from fair

Jessica?

LORENZO: I must needs tell thee all. She hath

directed

How I shall take her from her father's house,

What gold and jewels she is furnish'd with,

What page's suit she hath in readiness.

If e'er the Jew her father come to heaven,

It will be for his gentle daughter's sake:

And never dare misfortune cross her foot,

Unless she do it under this excuse,

That she is issue to a faithless Jew.

Come, go with me; peruse this as thou goest:

Fair Jessica shall be my torch-bearer.   [*Exeunt*]

SCENE V. The same. Before SHYLOCK'S house.

[*Enter SHYLOCK and LAUNCELOT*]

SHYLOCK: Well, thou shalt see, thy eyes shall

be thy judge,

The difference of old Shylock and Bassanio:–

What, Jessica!–thou shalt not gormandize,

As thou hast done with me: –What, Jessica!–

And sleep and snore, and rend apparel out; –

Why, Jessica, I say!

LAUNCELOT: Why, Jessica!

SHYLOCK: Who bids thee call? I do not bid thee call.

LAUNCELOT: Your worship was wont to tell me that I could do nothing without bidding.

[*Enter Jessica*]

JESSICA: Call you? what is your will?

SHYLOCK: I am bid forth to supper, Jessica:

There are my keys. But wherefore should I go?

I am not bid for love; they flatter me:

But yet I'll go in hate, to feed upon

The prodigal Christian. Jessica, my girl,

Look to my house. I am right loath to go:

There is some ill a-brewing towards my rest,

For I did dream of money-bags to-night.

LAUNCELOT: I beseech you, sir, go: my young master doth expect your reproach.

SHYLOCK: So do I his.

LAUNCELOT: And they have conspired together, I will not say you shall see a masque; but if you do, then it was not for nothing that my nose fell a-bleeding on Black-Monday last at six o'clock i' the morning, falling out that year on Ash-Wednesday was four year, in the afternoon.

SHYLOCK: What, are there masques? Hear you me, Jessica:

Lock up my doors; and when you hear the drum

And the vile squealing of the wry-neck'd fife,

Clamber not you up to the casements then,

Nor thrust your head into the public street

To gaze on Christian fools with varnish'd faces,

But stop my house's ears, I mean my casements:

Let not the sound of shallow foppery enter

My sober house. By Jacob's staff, I swear,

I have no mind of feasting forth to-night:

But I will go. Go you before me, sirrah;

Say I will come.

LAUNCELOT: I will go before, sir. Mistress, look out at window, for all this, There will come a Christian boy, will be worth a Jewess' eye.

[*Exit*]

SHYLOCK: What says that fool of Hagar's

offspring, ha?

JESSICA: His words were 'Farewell mistress;' nothing else.

SHYLOCK: The patch is kind enough, but a huge feeder;
Snail-slow in profit, and he sleeps by day
More than the wild-cat: drones hive not with me;
Therefore I part with him, and part with him
To one that would have him help to waste
His borrow'd purse. Well, Jessica, go in;
Perhaps I will return immediately:
Do as I bid you; shut doors after you:
Fast bind, fast find;
A proverb never stale in thrifty mind.
[*Exit*]

JESSICA: Farewell; and if my fortune be not crost,
I have a father, you a daughter, lost.
[*Exit*]

SCENE VI. The same.

[*Enter GRATIANO and SALARINO, masqued*]

GRATIANO: This is the pent-house under which

Lorenzo

Desired us to make stand.

SALARINO: His hour is almost past.

GRATIANO: And it is marvel he out-dwells his
hour,

For lovers ever run before the clock.

SALARINO: O, ten times faster Venus' pigeons
fly

To seal love's bonds new-made, than they are
wont

To keep obliged faith unforfeited!

GRATIANO: That ever holds: who riseth from a
feast

With that keen appetite that he sits down?

Where is the horse that doth untread again

His tedious measures with the unbated fire

That he did pace them first? All things that are,

Are with more spirit chased than enjoy'd.

How like a younker or a prodigal

The scarfed bark puts from her native bay,

Hugg'd and embraced by the strumpet wind!

How like the prodigal doth she return,

With over-weather'd ribs and ragged sails,

Lean, rent and beggar'd by the strumpet wind!

SALARINO: Here comes Lorenzo: more of this hereafter.

[*Enter LORENZO*]

LORENZO: Sweet friends, your patience for my long abode;

Not I, but my affairs, have made you wait:

When you shall please to play the thieves for wives,

I'll watch as long for you then. Approach;

Here dwells my father Jew. Ho! who's within?

[*Enter JESSICA, above, in boy's clothes*]

JESSICA: Who are you? Tell me, for more certainty,

Albeit I'll swear that I do know your tongue.

LORENZO: Lorenzo, and thy love.

JESSICA: Lorenzo, certain, and my love indeed,

For who love I so much? And now who knows

But you, Lorenzo, whether I am yours?

LORENZO: Heaven and thy thoughts are witness that thou art.

JESSICA: Here, catch this casket; it is worth the pains.

I am glad 'tis night, you do not look on me,

For I am much ashamed of my exchange:

But love is blind and lovers cannot see

The pretty follies that themselves commit;

For if they could, Cupid himself would blush

To see me thus transformed to a boy.

LORENZO: Descend, for you must be my

torchbearer.

JESSICA: What, must I hold a candle to my

shames?

They in themselves, good-sooth, are too too

light.

Why, 'tis an office of discovery, love;

And I should be obscured.

LORENZO: So are you, sweet,

Even in the lovely garnish of a boy.

But come at once;

For the close night doth play the runaway,

And we are stay'd for at Bassanio's feast.

JESSICA: I will make fast the doors, and gild

myself

With some more ducats, and be with you

straight.

[*Exit above*]

GRATIANO: Now, by my hood, a Gentile and no

Jew.

LORENZO: Beshrew me but I love her heartily;

For she is wise, if I can judge of her,

And fair she is, if that mine eyes be true,

And true she is, as she hath proved herself,

And therefore, like herself, wise, fair and true,

Shall she be placed in my constant soul.

[*Enter JESSICA, below*]

What, art thou come? On, gentlemen; away!

Our masquing mates by this time for us stay.

[*Exit with Jessica and Salarino*]

[*Enter ANTONIO*]

ANTONIO: Who's there?

GRATIANO: Signior Antonio!

ANTONIO: Fie, fie, Gratiano! where are all the rest?

'Tis nine o'clock: our friends all stay for you.

No masque to-night: the wind is come about;

Bassanio presently will go aboard:

I have sent twenty out to seek for you.

GRATIANO: I am glad on't: I desire no more delight

Than to be under sail and gone to-night.

[*Exeunt*]

SCENE VII. Belmont. A room in PORTIA'S house.

[*Flourish of cornets. Enter PORTIA, with the PRINCE OF MOROCCO, and their trains*]

PORTIA: Go draw aside the curtains and discover
The several caskets to this noble prince.
Now make your choice.

MOROCCO: The first, of gold, who this inscription bears,
'*Who chooseth me shall gain what many men desire*;'
The second, silver, which this promise carries,
'*Who chooseth me shall get as much as he deserves*;'
This third, dull lead, with warning all as blunt,
'*Who chooseth me must give and hazard all he hath*.'
How shall I know if I do choose the right?

PORTIA: The one of them contains my picture, prince:
If you choose that, then I am yours withal.

MOROCCO: Some god direct my judgment! Let

me see;

I will survey the inscriptions back again.

What says this leaden casket?

*'Who chooseth me must give and hazard all he
hath.'*

Must give: for what? for lead? hazard for lead?

This casket threatens. Men that hazard all

Do it in hope of fair advantages:

A golden mind stoops not to shows of dross;

I'll then nor give nor hazard aught for lead.

What says the silver with her virgin hue?

*'Who chooseth me shall get as much as he
deserves.'*

As much as he deserves! Pause there, Morocco,

And weigh thy value with an even hand:

If thou be'st rated by thy estimation,

Thou dost deserve enough; and yet enough

May not extend so far as to the lady:

And yet to be afeard of my deserving

Were but a weak disabling of myself.

As much as I deserve! Why, that's the lady:

I do in birth deserve her, and in fortunes,

In graces and in qualities of breeding;

But more than these, in love I do deserve.

What if I stray'd no further, but chose here?

Let's see once more this saying graved in gold

'Who chooseth me shall gain what many men

desire.'

Why, that's the lady; all the world desires her;

From the four corners of the earth they come,

To kiss this shrine, this mortal-breathing saint:

The Hyrcanian deserts and the vasty wilds

Of wide Arabia are as thoroughfares now

For princes to come view fair Portia:

The watery kingdom, whose ambitious head

Spits in the face of heaven, is no bar

To stop the foreign spirits, but they come,

As o'er a brook, to see fair Portia.

One of these three contains her heavenly

picture.

Is't like that lead contains her? 'Twere damnation

To think so base a thought: it were too gross

To rib her cerecloth in the obscure grave.

Or shall I think in silver she's immured,

Being ten times undervalued to tried gold?

O sinful thought! Never so rich a gem

Was set in worse than gold. They have in

England

A coin that bears the figure of an angel
Stamped in gold, but that's insculp'd upon;
But here an angel in a golden bed
Lies all within. Deliver me the key:
Here do I choose, and thrive I as I may!
PORTIA: There, take it, prince; and if my form lie there,
Then I am yours.

[*He unlocks the golden casket*]

MOROCCO: O hell! what have we here?
A carrion Death, within whose empty eye
There is a written scroll! I'll read the writing.

[*Reads*]

All that glitters is not gold;
Often have you heard that told:
Many a man his life hath sold
But my outside to behold:
Gilded tombs do worms enfold.
Had you been as wise as bold,
Young in limbs, in judgment old,
Your answer had not been inscroll'd:
Fare you well; your suit is cold.
Cold, indeed; and labour lost:
Then, farewell, heat, and welcome, frost!

Portia, adieu. I have too grieved a heart

To take a tedious leave: thus losers part.

[*Exit with his train. Flourish of cornets*]

PORTIA: A gentle riddance. Draw the curtains,

go.

Let all of his complexion choose me so.

[*Exeunt*]

SCENE VIII. Venice. A street.

[*Enter SALARINO and SALANIO*]

SALARINO: Why, man, I saw Bassanio under

sail:

With him is Gratiano gone along;

And in their ship I am sure Lorenzo is not.

SALANIO: The villain Jew with outcries raised

the duke,

Who went with him to search Bassanio's ship.

SALARINO: He came too late, the ship was

under sail:

But there the duke was given to understand

That in a gondola were seen together

Lorenzo and his amorous Jessica:

Besides, Antonio certified the duke

They were not with Bassanio in his ship.

SALANIO: I never heard a passion so confused,

So strange, outrageous, and so variable,

As the dog Jew did utter in the streets:

'My daughter! O my ducats! O my daughter!

Fled with a Christian! O my Christian ducats!

Justice! the law! my ducats, and my daughter!

A sealed bag, two sealed bags of ducats,

Of double ducats, stolen from me by my

daughter!

And jewels, two stones, two rich and precious

stones,

Stolen by my daughter! Justice! find the girl;

She hath the stones upon her, and the ducats.'

SALARINO: Why, all the boys in Venice follow

him,

Crying, his stones, his daughter, and his ducats.

SALANIO: Let good Antonio look he keep his

day,

Or he shall pay for this.

SALARINO: Marry, well remember'd.

I reason'd with a Frenchman yesterday,

Who told me, in the narrow seas that part

The French and English, there miscarried

A vessel of our country richly fraught:

I thought upon Antonio when he told me;

And wish'd in silence that it were not his.

SALANIO: You were best to tell Antonio what

you hear;

Yet do not suddenly, for it may grieve him.

SALARINO: A kinder gentleman treads not the

earth.

I saw Bassanio and Antonio part:

Bassanio told him he would make some speed

Of his return: he answer'd, 'Do not so;

Slubber not business for my sake, Bassanio

But stay the very riping of the time;

And for the Jew's bond which he hath of me,

Let it not enter in your mind of love:

Be merry, and employ your chiefest thoughts

To courtship and such fair ostents of love

As shall conveniently become you there:'

And even there, his eye being big with tears,

Turning his face, he put his hand behind him,

And with affection wondrous sensible

He wrung Bassanio's hand; and so they parted.

SALANIO: I think he only loves the world for

him.

I pray thee, let us go and find him out

And quicken his embraced heaviness

With some delight or other.

SALARINO: Do we so.

[*Exeunt*]

SCENE IX. Belmont. A room in PORTIA'S house.

[*Enter NERISSA with a Servitor*]

NERISSA: Quick, quick, I pray thee; draw the curtain straight:

The Prince of Arragon hath ta'en his oath,

And comes to his election presently.

[*Flourish of cornets. Enter the PRINCE OF ARRAGON, PORTIA, and their trains*]

PORTIA: Behold, there stand the caskets, noble prince:

If you choose that wherein I am contain'd,

Straight shall our nuptial rites be solemnized:

But if you fail, without more speech, my lord,

You must be gone from hence immediately.

ARRAGON: I am enjoin'd by oath to observe three things:

First, never to unfold to any one

Which casket 'twas I chose; next, if I fail

Of the right casket, never in my life

To woo a maid in way of marriage: Lastly,

If I do fail in fortune of my choice,

Immediately to leave you and be gone.

PORTIA: To these injunctions every one doth swear

That comes to hazard for my worthless self.

ARRAGON: And so have I address'd me.

Fortune now

To my heart's hope! Gold; silver; and base lead.

'Who chooseth me must give and hazard all he hath.'

You shall look fairer, ere I give or hazard.

What says the golden chest? ha! let me see:

'Who chooseth me shall gain what many men desire.'

What many men desire! that 'many' may be meant

By the fool multitude, that choose by show,

Not learning more than the fond eye doth teach;

Which pries not to the interior, but, like the martlet,

Builds in the weather on the outward wall,
Even in the force and road of casualty.
I will not choose what many men desire,
Because I will not jump with common spirits
And rank me with the barbarous multitudes.
Why, then to thee, thou silver treasure-house;
Tell me once more what title thou dost bear:
'Who chooseth me shall get as much as he
deserves:'
And well said too; for who shall go about
To cozen fortune and be honourable
Without the stamp of merit? Let none presume
To wear an undeserved dignity.
O, that estates, degrees and offices
Were not derived corruptly, and that clear honour
Were purchased by the merit of the wearer!
How many then should cover that stand bare!
How many be commanded that command!
How much low peasantry would then be glean'd
From the true seed of honour! and how much
honour
Pick'd from the chaff and ruin of the times
To be new-varnish'd! Well, but to my choice:
'Who chooseth me shall get as much as he

deserves.'

I will assume desert. Give me a key for this,

And instantly unlock my fortunes here.

[*He opens the silver casket*]

PORTIA: Too long a pause for that which you find there.

ARRAGON: What's here? the portrait of a blinking idiot,

Presenting me a schedule! I will read it.

How much unlike art thou to Portia!

How much unlike my hopes and my deservings!

'Who chooseth me shall have as much as he deserves.'

Did I deserve no more than a fool's head?

Is that my prize? are my deserts no better?

PORTIA: To offend, and judge, are distinct offices

And of opposed natures.

ARRAGON: What is here? [*Reads*]

The fire seven times tried this:

Seven times tried that judgment is,

That did never choose amiss.

Some there be that shadows kiss;

Such have but a shadow's bliss:

There be fools alive, I wis,

Silver'd o'er; and so was this.

Take what wife you will to bed,

I will ever be your head:

So be gone: you are sped.

Still more fool I shall appear

By the time I linger here

With one fool's head I came to woo,

But I go away with two.

Sweet, adieu. I'll keep my oath,

Patiently to bear my wroth.

[*Exeunt Arragon and train*]

PORTIA: Thus hath the candle singed the moth.

O, these deliberate fools! when they do choose,

They have the wisdom by their wit to lose.

NERISSA: The ancient saying is no heresy,

Hanging and wiving goes by destiny.

PORTIA: Come, draw the curtain, Nerissa.

[*Enter a Servant*]

Servant: Where is my lady?

PORTIA: Here: what would my lord?

Servant: Madam, there is alighted at your gate

A young Venetian, one that comes before

To signify the approaching of his lord;

From whom he bringeth sensible regreets,

To wit, besides commends and courteous
breath,

Gifts of rich value. Yet I have not seen

So likely an ambassador of love:

A day in April never came so sweet,

To show how costly summer was at hand,

As this fore-spurrer comes before his lord.

PORTIA: No more, I pray thee: I am half afeard

Thou wilt say anon he is some kin to thee,

Thou spend'st such high-day wit in praising him.

Come, come, Nerissa; for I long to see

Quick Cupid's post that comes so mannerly.

NERISSA: Bassanio, lord Love, if thy will it be!

[*Exeunt*]

My Notes

ACT III

SCENE I. Venice. A street.

[*Enter SALANIO and SALARINO*]

SALANIO: Now, what news on the Rialto?

SALARINO: Why, yet it lives there uncheck'd that Antonio hath a ship of rich lading wrecked on the narrow seas; the Goodwins, I think they call the place; a very dangerous flat and fatal, where the carcasses of many a tall ship lie buried, as they say, if my gossip Report be an honest woman of her word.

SALANIO: I would she were as lying a gossip in that as ever knapped ginger or made her neighbours believe she wept for the death of a third husband. But it is true, without any slips of prolixity or crossing the plain highway of talk, that the good Antonio, the honest Antonio, –O that I had a title good enough to keep his name company!–

SALARINO: Come, the full stop.

SALANIO: Ha! what sayest thou? Why, the end is, he hath

lost a ship.

SALARINO: I would it might prove the end of his losses.

SALANIO: Let me say 'amen' betimes, lest the devil cross my prayer, for here he comes in the likeness of a Jew.

[*Enter SHYLOCK*]

How now, Shylock! what news among the merchants?

SHYLOCK: You know, none so well, none so well as you, of my daughter's flight.

SALARINO: That's certain: I, for my part, knew the tailor that made the wings she flew withal.

SALANIO: And Shylock, for his own part, knew the bird was fledged; and then it is the complexion of them all to leave the dam.

SHYLOCK: She is damned for it.

SALANIO: That's certain, if the devil may be her judge.

SHYLOCK: My own flesh and blood to rebel!

SALANIO: Out upon it, old carrion! rebels it at these years?

SHYLOCK: I say, my daughter is my flesh and blood.

SALARINO: There is more difference between thy flesh and hers than between jet and ivory; more between your bloods than there is between red wine and rhenish. But tell us, do you hear whether Antonio have had any loss at sea or no?

SHYLOCK: There I have another bad match: a bankrupt, a prodigal, who dare scarce show his head on the Rialto; a beggar, that was used to come so smug upon the mart; let him look to his bond: he was wont to call me usurer; let him look to his bond: he was wont to lend money for a Christian courtesy; let him look to his bond.

SALARINO: Why, I am sure, if he forfeit, thou wilt not take his flesh: what's that good for?

SHYLOCK: To bait fish withal: if it will feed nothing else, it will feed my revenge. He hath disgraced me, and hindered me half a million; laughed at my losses, mocked at my gains, scorned my nation, thwarted my bargains, cooled my friends, heated mine enemies; and what's his reason? I am a Jew. Hath not a Jew eyes? hath not a Jew hands, organs, dimensions, senses, affections, passions? fed with the same food, hurt with the same weapons, subject to the same diseases, healed by the same means, warmed and cooled by the same winter and summer, as a Christian is? If you prick us, do we not bleed? if you tickle us, do we not laugh? if you poison us, do we not die? and if you wrong us, shall we not revenge? If we are like you in the rest, we will resemble you in that. If a Jew wrong a Christian, what is his humility? Revenge. If a Christian wrong a Jew, what should his sufferance be by Christian example? Why, revenge. The villany you teach me, I will execute, and it shall go hard but I will better the instruction.

[*Enter a Servant*]

Servant: Gentlemen, my master Antonio is at his house and desires to speak with you both.

SALARINO: We have been up and down to seek him.

[*Enter TUBAL*]

SALANIO: Here comes another of the tribe: a third cannot be matched, unless the devil himself turn Jew.

[*Exeunt SALANIO, SALARINO, and Servant*]

SHYLOCK: How now, Tubal! what news from Genoa? hast thou found my daughter?

TUBAL: I often came where I did hear of her, but cannot find her.

SHYLOCK: Why, there, there, there, there! a diamond gone, cost me two thousand ducats in Frankfort! The curse never fell upon our nation till now; I never felt it till now: two thousand ducats in that; and other precious, precious jewels. I would my daughter were dead at my foot, and the jewels in her ear! would she were hearsed at my foot, and the ducats in her coffin! No news of them? Why, so: and I know not what's spent in the search: why, thou loss upon loss! the thief gone with so much, and so much to find the thief; and no satisfaction, no revenge: nor no in luck stirring but what lights on my shoulders; no sighs but of my breathing; no tears but of my shedding.

TUBAL: Yes, other men have ill luck too: Antonio, as I heard in Genoa, –

SHYLOCK: What, what, what? ill luck, ill luck?

TUBAL: Hath an argosy cast away, coming from Tripolis.

SHYLOCK: I thank God, I thank God. Is't true, is't true?

TUBAL: I spoke with some of the sailors that

escaped the wreck.

SHYLOCK: I thank thee, good Tubal: good news, good news! ha, ha! where? in Genoa?

TUBAL: Your daughter spent in Genoa, as I heard, in one night fourscore ducats.

SHYLOCK: Thou stickest a dagger in me: I shall never see my gold again: fourscore ducats at a sitting! fourscore ducats!

TUBAL: There came divers of Antonio's creditors in my company to Venice, that swear he cannot choose but break.

SHYLOCK: I am very glad of it: I'll plague him; I'll torture him: I am glad of it.

TUBAL: One of them showed me a ring that he had of your daughter for a monkey.

SHYLOCK: Out upon her! Thou torturest me, Tubal: it was my turquoise; I had it of Leah when I was a bachelor: I would not have given it for a wilderness of monkeys.

TUBAL: But Antonio is certainly undone.

SHYLOCK: Nay, that's true, that's very true. Go, Tubal, fee me an officer; bespeak him a fortnight before. I will have the heart of him, if he forfeit; for, were he out of Venice, I can make what

merchandise I will. Go, go, Tubal, and meet me
at our synagogue; go, good Tubal; at our
synagogue, Tubal.
[*Exeunt*]

SCENE II. Belmont. A room in PORTIA'S house.

[*Enter BASSANIO, PORTIA, GRATIANO,*
NERISSA, and Attendants]

PORTIA: I pray you, tarry: pause a day or two
Before you hazard; for, in choosing wrong,
I lose your company: therefore forbear awhile.
There's something tells me, but it is not love,
I would not lose you; and you know yourself,
Hate counsels not in such a quality.
But lest you should not understand me well, –
And yet a maiden hath no tongue but thought,–
I would detain you here some month or two
Before you venture for me. I could teach you
How to choose right, but I am then forsworn;
So will I never be: so may you miss me;
But if you do, you'll make me wish a sin,
That I had been forsworn. Beshrew your eyes,

They have o'erlook'd me and divided me;

One half of me is yours, the other half yours,

Mine own, I would say; but if mine, then yours,

And so all yours. O, these naughty times

Put bars between the owners and their rights!

And so, though yours, not yours. Prove it so,

Let fortune go to hell for it, not I.

I speak too long; but 'tis to peise the time,

To eke it and to draw it out in length,

To stay you from election.

BASSANIO: Let me choose

For as I am, I live upon the rack.

PORTIA: Upon the rack, Bassanio! then confess

What treason there is mingled with your love.

BASSANIO: None but that ugly treason of

mistrust,

Which makes me fear the enjoying of my love:

There may as well be amity and life

'Tween snow and fire, as treason and my love.

PORTIA: Ay, but I fear you speak upon the rack,

Where men enforced do speak anything.

BASSANIO: Promise me life, and I'll confess the

truth.

PORTIA: Well then, confess and live.

BASSANIO: 'Confess' and 'love'

Had been the very sum of my confession:

O happy torment, when my torturer

Doth teach me answers for deliverance!

But let me to my fortune and the caskets.

PORTIA: Away, then! I am lock'd in one of them:

If you do love me, you will find me out.

Nerissa and the rest, stand all aloof.

Let music sound while he doth make his choice;

Then, if he lose, he makes a swan-like end,

Fading in music: that the comparison

May stand more proper, my eye shall be the
stream

And watery death-bed for him. He may win;

And what is music then? Then music is

Even as the flourish when true subjects bow

To a new-crowned monarch: such it is

As are those dulcet sounds in break of day

That creep into the dreaming bridegroom's ear,

And summon him to marriage. Now he goes,

With no less presence, but with much more love,

Than young Alcides, when he did redeem

The virgin tribute paid by howling Troy

To the sea-monster: I stand for sacrifice

The rest aloof are the Dardanian wives,
With bleared visages, come forth to view
The issue of the exploit. Go, Hercules!
Live thou, I live: with much, much more dismay
I view the fight than thou that makest the fray.
[*Music, whilst BASSANIO comments on the
caskets to himself*]
[SONG.]
Tell me where is fancy bred,
Or in the heart, or in the head?
How begot, how nourished?
Reply, reply.
It is engender'd in the eyes,
With gazing fed; and fancy dies
In the cradle where it lies.
Let us all ring fancy's knell
I'll begin it,–Ding, dong, bell.
ALL: *Ding, dong, bell.*
BASSANIO: So may the outward shows be least
themselves:
The world is still deceived with ornament.
In law, what plea so tainted and corrupt,
But, being seasoned with a gracious voice,
Obscures the show of evil? In religion,

What damned error, but some sober brow
Will bless it and approve it with a text,
Hiding the grossness with fair ornament?
There is no vice so simple but assumes
Some mark of virtue on his outward parts:
How many cowards, whose hearts are all as
false
As stairs of sand, wear yet upon their chins
The beards of Hercules and frowning Mars;
Who, inward search'd, have livers white as milk;
And these assume but valour's excrement
To render them redoubted! Look on beauty,
And you shall see 'tis purchased by the weight;
Which therein works a miracle in nature,
Making them lightest that wear most of it:
So are those crisped snaky golden locks
Which make such wanton gambols with the wind,
Upon supposed fairness, often known
To be the dowry of a second head,
The skull that bred them in the sepulchre.
Thus ornament is but the guiled shore
To a most dangerous sea; the beauteous scarf
Veiling an Indian beauty; in a word,
The seeming truth which cunning times put on

To entrap the wisest. Therefore, thou gaudy gold,
Hard food for Midas, I will none of thee;
Nor none of thee, thou pale and common drudge
'Tween man and man: but thou, thou meagre lead,
Which rather threatenest than dost promise aught,
Thy paleness moves me more than eloquence;
And here choose I; joy be the consequence!
PORTIA: [Aside] How all the other passions fleet to air,
As doubtful thoughts, and rash-embraced despair,
And shuddering fear, and green-eyed jealousy!
O love,
Be moderate; allay thy ecstasy,
In measure rein thy joy; scant this excess.
I feel too much thy blessing: make it less,
For fear I surfeit.
BASSANIO: What find I here?
[*Opening the leaden casket*]
Fair Portia's counterfeit! What demi-god
Hath come so near creation? Move these eyes?

Or whether, riding on the balls of mine,
Seem they in motion? Here are sever'd lips,
Parted with sugar breath: so sweet a bar
Should sunder such sweet friends. Here in her
hairs
The painter plays the spider and hath woven
A golden mesh to entrap the hearts of men,
Faster than gnats in cobwebs; but her eyes,—
How could he see to do them? having made one,
Methinks it should have power to steal both his
And leave itself unfurnish'd. Yet look, how far
The substance of my praise doth wrong this
shadow
In underprizing it, so far this shadow
Doth limp behind the substance. Here's the
scroll,
The continent and summary of my fortune.
[*Reads*]
You that choose not by the view,
Chance as fair and choose as true!
Since this fortune falls to you,
Be content and seek no new,
If you be well pleased with this
And hold your fortune for your bliss,

Turn you where your lady is
And claim her with a loving kiss.
A gentle scroll. Fair lady, by your leave;
[*Kissing her*] I come by note, to give and to
receive.
Like one of two contending in a prize,
That thinks he hath done well in people's eyes,
Hearing applause and universal shout,
Giddy in spirit, still gazing in a doubt
Whether these pearls of praise be his or no;
So, thrice fair lady, stand I, even so;
As doubtful whether what I see be true,
Until confirm'd, sign'd, ratified by you.
PORTIA: You see me, Lord Bassanio, where I
stand,
Such as I am: though for myself alone
I would not be ambitious in my wish,
To wish myself much better; yet, for you
I would be trebled twenty times myself;
A thousand times more fair, ten thousand times
more rich;
That only to stand high in your account,
I might in virtue, beauties, livings, friends,
Exceed account; but the full sum of me

Is sum of something, which, to term in gross,

Is an unlesson'd girl, unschool'd, unpractised;

Happy in this, she is not yet so old

But she may learn; happier than this,

She is not bred so dull but she can learn;

Happiest of all is that her gentle spirit

Commits itself to yours to be directed,

As from her lord, her governor, her king.

Myself and what is mine to you and yours

Is now converted: but now I was the lord

Of this fair mansion, master of my servants,

Queen o'er myself: and even now, but now,

This house, these servants and this same myself

Are yours, my lord: I give them with this ring;

Which when you part from, lose, or give away,

Let it presage the ruin of your love

And be my vantage to exclaim on you.

BASSANIO: Madam, you have bereft me of all words,

Only my blood speaks to you in my veins;

And there is such confusion in my powers,

As after some oration fairly spoke

By a beloved prince, there doth appear

Among the buzzing pleased multitude;

Where every something, being blent together,

Turns to a wild of nothing, save of joy,

Express'd and not express'd. But when this ring

Parts from this finger, then parts life from hence:

O, then be bold to say Bassanio's dead!

NERISSA: My lord and lady, it is now our time,

That have stood by and seen our wishes

prosper,

To cry, good joy: good joy, my lord and lady!

GRATIANO: My lord Bassanio and my gentle

lady,

I wish you all the joy that you can wish;

For I am sure you can wish none from me:

And when your honours mean to solemnize

The bargain of your faith, I do beseech you,

Even at that time I may be married too.

BASSANIO: With all my heart, so thou canst get

a wife.

GRATIANO: I thank your lordship, you have got

me one.

My eyes, my lord, can look as swift as yours:

You saw the mistress, I beheld the maid;

You loved, I loved for intermission.

No more pertains to me, my lord, than you.

Your fortune stood upon the casket there,

And so did mine too, as the matter falls;

For wooing here until I sweat again,

And sweating until my very roof was dry

With oaths of love, at last, if promise last,

I got a promise of this fair one here

To have her love, provided that your fortune

Achieved her mistress.

PORTIA: Is this true, Nerissa?

NERISSA: Madam, it is, so you stand pleased
withal.

BASSANIO: And do you, Gratiano, mean good
faith?

GRATIANO: Yes, faith, my lord.

BASSANIO: Our feast shall be much honour'd in
your marriage.

GRATIANO: We'll play with them the first boy for
a thousand ducats.

NERISSA: What, and stake down?

GRATIANO: No; we shall ne'er win at that sport,
and stake down.

But who comes here? Lorenzo and his infidel?

What, and my old Venetian friend Salerio?

[*Enter LORENZO, JESSICA, and SALERIO, a*

Messenger from Venice]

BASSANIO: Lorenzo and Salerio, welcome hither;

If that the youth of my new interest here

Have power to bid you welcome. By your leave,

I bid my very friends and countrymen,

Sweet Portia, welcome.

PORTIA: So do I, my lord:

They are entirely welcome.

LORENZO: I thank your honour. For my part, my lord,

My purpose was not to have seen you here;

But meeting with Salerio by the way,

He did entreat me, past all saying nay,

To come with him along.

SALERIO: I did, my lord;

And I have reason for it. Signior Antonio

Commends him to you.

[*Gives Bassanio a letter*]

BASSANIO: Ere I ope his letter,

I pray you, tell me how my good friend doth.

SALERIO: Not sick, my lord, unless it be in mind;

Nor well, unless in mind: his letter there

Will show you his estate.

GRATIANO: Nerissa, cheer yon stranger; bid
her welcome.

Your hand, Salerio: what's the news from
Venice?

How doth that royal merchant, good Antonio?

I know he will be glad of our success;

We are the Jasons, we have won the fleece.

SALERIO: I would you had won the fleece that
he hath lost.

PORTIA: There are some shrewd contents in
yon same paper,

That steals the colour from Bassanio's cheek:

Some dear friend dead; else nothing in the world

Could turn so much the constitution

Of any constant man. What, worse and worse!

With leave, Bassanio: I am half yourself,

And I must freely have the half of anything

That this same paper brings you.

BASSANIO: O sweet Portia,

Here are a few of the unpleasant'st words

That ever blotted paper! Gentle lady,

When I did first impart my love to you,

I freely told you, all the wealth I had

Ran in my veins, I was a gentleman;
And then I told you true: and yet, dear lady,
Rating myself at nothing, you shall see
How much I was a braggart. When I told you
My state was nothing, I should then have told you
That I was worse than nothing; for, indeed,
I have engaged myself to a dear friend,
Engaged my friend to his mere enemy,
To feed my means. Here is a letter, lady;
The paper as the body of my friend,
And every word in it a gaping wound,
Issuing life-blood. But is it true, Salerio?
Have all his ventures fail'd? What, not one hit?
From Tripolis, from Mexico and England,
From Lisbon, Barbary and India?
And not one vessel 'scape the dreadful touch
Of merchant-marring rocks?

SALERIO: Not one, my lord.
Besides, it should appear, that if he had
The present money to discharge the Jew,
He would not take it. Never did I know
A creature, that did bear the shape of man,
So keen and greedy to confound a man:

He plies the duke at morning and at night,

And doth impeach the freedom of the state,

If they deny him justice: twenty merchants,

The duke himself, and the magnificoes

Of greatest port, have all persuaded with him;

But none can drive him from the envious plea

Of forfeiture, of justice and his bond.

JESSICA: When I was with him I have heard him swear

To Tubal and to Chus, his countrymen,

That he would rather have Antonio's flesh

Than twenty times the value of the sum

That he did owe him: and I know, my lord,

If law, authority and power deny not,

It will go hard with poor Antonio.

PORTIA: Is it your dear friend that is thus in trouble?

BASSANIO: The dearest friend to me, the kindest man,

The best-condition'd and unwearied spirit

In doing courtesies, and one in whom

The ancient Roman honour more appears

Than any that draws breath in Italy.

PORTIA: What sum owes he the Jew?

BASSANIO: For me three thousand ducats.

PORTIA: What, no more?

Pay him six thousand, and deface the bond;

Double six thousand, and then treble that,

Before a friend of this description

Shall lose a hair through Bassanio's fault.

First go with me to church and call me wife,

And then away to Venice to your friend;

For never shall you lie by Portia's side

With an unquiet soul. You shall have gold

To pay the petty debt twenty times over:

When it is paid, bring your true friend along.

My maid Nerissa and myself meantime

Will live as maids and widows. Come, away!

For you shall hence upon your wedding-day:

Bid your friends welcome, show a merry cheer:

Since you are dear bought, I will love you dear.

But let me hear the letter of your friend.

BASSANIO: [Reads] Sweet Bassanio, my ships have all miscarried, my creditors grow cruel, my estate is very low, my bond to the Jew is forfeit; and since in paying it, it is impossible I should live, all debts are cleared between you and I, if I might but see you at my death. Notwithstanding,

use your pleasure: if your love do not persuade
you to come, let not my letter.

PORTIA: O love, dispatch all business, and be
gone!

BASSANIO: Since I have your good leave to go
away,
I will make haste: but, till I come again,
No bed shall e'er be guilty of my stay,
No rest be interposer 'twixt us twain.
[*Exeunt*]

SCENE III. Venice. A street.

[*Enter SHYLOCK, SALARINO, ANTONIO, and
Gaoler*]

SHYLOCK: Gaoler, look to him: tell not me of
mercy;
This is the fool that lent out money gratis:
Gaoler, look to him.

ANTONIO: Hear me yet, good Shylock.

SHYLOCK: I'll have my bond; speak not against
my bond:
I have sworn an oath that I will have my bond.
Thou call'dst me dog before thou hadst a cause;

But, since I am a dog, beware my fangs:

The duke shall grant me justice. I do wonder,

Thou naughty gaoler, that thou art so fond

To come abroad with him at his request.

ANTONIO: I pray thee, hear me speak.

SHYLOCK: I'll have my bond; I will not hear thee

speak:

I'll have my bond; and therefore speak no more.

I'll not be made a soft and dull-eyed fool,

To shake the head, relent, and sigh, and yield

To Christian intercessors. Follow not;

I'll have no speaking: I will have my bond.

[*Exit*]

SALARINO: It is the most impenetrable cur

That ever kept with men.

ANTONIO: Let him alone:

I'll follow him no more with bootless prayers.

He seeks my life; his reason well I know:

I oft deliver'd from his forfeitures

Many that have at times made moan to me;

Therefore he hates me.

SALARINO: I am sure the duke

Will never grant this forfeiture to hold.

ANTONIO: The duke cannot deny the course of

law:

For the commodity that strangers have

With us in Venice, if it be denied,

Will much impeach the justice of his state;

Since that the trade and profit of the city

Consisteth of all nations. Therefore, go:

These griefs and losses have so bated me,

That I shall hardly spare a pound of flesh

To-morrow to my bloody creditor.

Well, gaoler, on. Pray God, Bassanio come

To see me pay his debt, and then I care not!

[*Exeunt*]

SCENE IV. Belmont. A room in PORTIA'S house.

[*Enter PORTIA, NERISSA, LORENZO, JESSICA, and BALTHASAR*]

LORENZO: Madam, although I speak it in your presence,

You have a noble and a true conceit

Of godlike amity; which appears most strongly

In bearing thus the absence of your lord.

But if you knew to whom you show this honour,

How true a gentleman you send relief,

How dear a lover of my lord your husband,

I know you would be prouder of the work

Than customary bounty can enforce you.

PORTIA: I never did repent for doing good,

Nor shall not now: for in companions

That do converse and waste the time together,

Whose souls do bear an equal yoke of love,

There must be needs a like proportion

Of lineaments, of manners and of spirit;

Which makes me think that this Antonio,

Being the bosom lover of my lord,

Must needs be like my lord. If it be so,

How little is the cost I have bestow'd

In purchasing the semblance of my soul

From out the state of hellish misery!

This comes too near the praising of myself;

Therefore no more of it: hear other things.

Lorenzo, I commit into your hands

The husbandry and manage of my house

Until my lord's return: for mine own part,

I have toward heaven breathed a secret vow

To live in prayer and contemplation,

Only attended by Nerissa here,

Until her husband and my lord's return:

There is a monastery two miles off;

And there will we abide. I do desire you

Not to deny this imposition;

The which my love and some necessity

Now lays upon you.

LORENZO: Madam, with all my heart;

I shall obey you in all fair commands.

PORTIA: My people do already know my mind,

And will acknowledge you and Jessica

In place of Lord Bassanio and myself.

And so farewell, till we shall meet again.

LORENZO: Fair thoughts and happy hours

attend on you!

JESSICA: I wish your ladyship all heart's

content.

PORTIA: I thank you for your wish, and am well

pleased

To wish it back on you: fare you well Jessica.

[*Exeunt JESSICA and LORENZO*]

Now, Balthasar,

As I have ever found thee honest-true,

So let me find thee still. Take this same letter,

And use thou all the endeavour of a man

In speed to Padua: see thou render this
Into my cousin's hand, Doctor Bellario;
And, look, what notes and garments he doth give
thee,
Bring them, I pray thee, with imagined speed
Unto the tranect, to the common ferry
Which trades to Venice. Waste no time in words,
But get thee gone: I shall be there before thee.
BALTHASAR: Madam, I go with all convenient
speed.
[*Exit*]
PORTIA: Come on, Nerissa; I have work in hand
That you yet know not of: we'll see our husbands
Before they think of us.
NERISSA: Shall they see us?
PORTIA: They shall, Nerissa; but in such a
habit,
That they shall think we are accomplished
With that we lack. I'll hold thee any wager,
When we are both accoutred like young men,
I'll prove the prettier fellow of the two,
And wear my dagger with the braver grace,
And speak between the change of man and boy
With a reed voice, and turn two mincing steps

Into a manly stride, and speak of frays
Like a fine bragging youth, and tell quaint lies,
How honourable ladies sought my love,
Which I denying, they fell sick and died;
I could not do withal; then I'll repent,
And wish for all that, that I had not killed them;
And twenty of these puny lies I'll tell,
That men shall swear I have discontinued school
Above a twelvemonth. I have within my mind
A thousand raw tricks of these bragging Jacks,
Which I will practise.
NERISSA: Why, shall we turn to men?
PORTIA: Fie, what a question's that,
If thou wert near a lewd interpreter!
But come, I'll tell thee all my whole device
When I am in my coach, which stays for us
At the park gate; and therefore haste away,
For we must measure twenty miles to-day.
[*Exeunt*]

SCENE V. The same. A garden.

[*Enter LAUNCELOT and JESSICA*]
LAUNCELOT: Yes, truly; for, look you, the sins

of the father are to be laid upon the children: therefore, I promise ye, I fear you. I was always plain with you, and so now I speak my agitation of the matter: therefore be of good cheer, for truly I think you are damned. There is but one hope in it that can do you any good; and that is but a kind of bastard hope neither.

JESSICA: And what hope is that, I pray thee?

LAUNCELOT: Marry, you may partly hope that your father got you not, that you are not the Jew's daughter.

JESSICA: That were a kind of bastard hope, indeed: so the sins of my mother should be visited upon me.

LAUNCELOT: Truly then I fear you are damned both by father and mother: thus when I shun Scylla, your father, I fall into Charybdis, your mother: well, you are gone both ways.

JESSICA: I shall be saved by my husband; he hath made me a Christian.

LAUNCELOT: Truly, the more to blame he: we were Christians enow before; e'en as many as could well live, one by another. This making Christians will raise the price of hogs: if we grow all to be pork-eaters, we shall not shortly have a rasher on the coals for money.

[Enter LORENZO]

JESSICA: I'll tell my husband, Launcelot, what you say: here he comes.

LORENZO: I shall grow jealous of you shortly, Launcelot, if you thus get my wife into corners.

JESSICA: Nay, you need not fear us, Lorenzo: Launcelot and I are out. He tells me flatly, there is no mercy for me in heaven, because I am a Jew's daughter: and he says, you are no good member of the commonwealth, for in converting Jews to Christians, you raise the price of pork.

LORENZO: I shall answer that better to the commonwealth than you can the getting up of the negro's belly: the Moor is with child by you, Launcelot.

LAUNCELOT: It is much that the Moor should be more than reason: but if she be less than an honest woman, she is indeed more than I took her for.

LORENZO: How every fool can play upon the word! I think the best grace of wit will shortly turn into silence, and discourse grow commendable in none only but parrots. Go in, sirrah; bid them prepare for dinner.

LAUNCELOT: That is done, sir; they have all stomachs.

LORENZO: Goodly Lord, what a wit-snapper are you! then bid them prepare dinner.

LAUNCELOT: That is done too, sir; only 'cover' is the word.

LORENZO: Will you cover then, sir?

LAUNCELOT: Not so, sir, neither; I know my duty.

LORENZO: Yet more quarrelling with occasion! Wilt thou show the whole wealth of thy wit in an instant? I pray tree, understand a plain man in his plain meaning: go to thy fellows; bid them cover the table, serve in the meat, and we will come in to dinner.

LAUNCELOT: For the table, sir, it shall be served in; for the meat, sir, it shall be covered; for your coming in to dinner, sir, why, let it be as humours and conceits shall govern.

[*Exit*]

LORENZO: O dear discretion, how his words are suited!

The fool hath planted in his memory
An army of good words; and I do know
A many fools, that stand in better place,
Garnish'd like him, that for a tricksy word
Defy the matter. How cheerest thou, Jessica?
And now, good sweet, say thy opinion,
How dost thou like the Lord Bassanio's wife?

JESSICA: Past all expressing. It is very meet
The Lord Bassanio live an upright life;
For, having such a blessing in his lady,
He finds the joys of heaven here on earth;
And if on earth he do not mean it, then
In reason he should never come to heaven
Why, if two gods should play some heavenly
match
And on the wager lay two earthly women,
And Portia one, there must be something else
Pawn'd with the other, for the poor rude world
Hath not her fellow.

LORENZO: Even such a husband
Hast thou of me as she is for a wife.

JESSICA: Nay, but ask my opinion too of that.

LORENZO: I will anon: first, let us go to dinner.

JESSICA: Nay, let me praise you while I have a

stomach.

LORENZO: No, pray thee, let it serve for table-talk;

Then, howso'er thou speak'st, 'mong other things I shall digest it.

JESSICA: Well, I'll set you forth.

[*Exeunt*]

My Notes

ACT IV

SCENE I. Venice. A court of justice.

[*Enter the DUKE, the Magnificoes, ANTONIO, BASSANIO, GRATIANO, SALERIO, and others*]

DUKE: What, is Antonio here?

ANTONIO: Ready, so please your grace.

DUKE: I am sorry for thee: thou art come to answer

A stony adversary, an inhuman wretch

uncapable of pity, void and empty

From any dram of mercy.

ANTONIO: I have heard

Your grace hath ta'en great pains to qualify

His rigorous course; but since he stands obdurate

And that no lawful means can carry me

Out of his envy's reach, I do oppose

My patience to his fury, and am arm'd

To suffer, with a quietness of spirit,

The very tyranny and rage of his.

DUKE: Go one, and call the Jew into the court.

SALERIO: He is ready at the door: he comes,

my lord.

[*Enter SHYLOCK*]

DUKE: Make room, and let him stand before our face.

Shylock, the world thinks, and I think so too,

That thou but lead'st this fashion of thy malice

To the last hour of act; and then 'tis thought

Thou'lt show thy mercy and remorse more strange

Than is thy strange apparent cruelty;

And where thou now exact'st the penalty,

Which is a pound of this poor merchant's flesh,

Thou wilt not only loose the forfeiture,

But, touch'd with human gentleness and love,

Forgive a moiety of the principal;

Glancing an eye of pity on his losses,

That have of late so huddled on his back,

Enow to press a royal merchant down

And pluck commiseration of his state

From brassy bosoms and rough hearts of flint,

From stubborn Turks and Tartars, never train'd

To offices of tender courtesy.

We all expect a gentle answer, Jew.

SHYLOCK: I have possess'd your grace of what

I purpose;

And by our holy Sabbath have I sworn

To have the due and forfeit of my bond:

If you deny it, let the danger light

Upon your charter and your city's freedom.

You'll ask me, why I rather choose to have

A weight of carrion flesh than to receive

Three thousand ducats: I'll not answer that:

But, say, it is my humour: is it answer'd?

What if my house be troubled with a rat

And I be pleased to give ten thousand ducats

To have it baned? What, are you answer'd yet?

Some men there are love not a gaping pig;

Some, that are mad if they behold a cat;

And others, when the bagpipe sings i' the nose,

Cannot contain their urine: for affection,

Mistress of passion, sways it to the mood

Of what it likes or loathes. Now, for your answer:

As there is no firm reason to be render'd,

Why he cannot abide a gaping pig;

Why he, a harmless necessary cat;

Why he, a woollen bagpipe; but of force

Must yield to such inevitable shame

As to offend, himself being offended;

So can I give no reason, nor I will not,
More than a lodged hate and a certain loathing
I bear Antonio, that I follow thus
A losing suit against him. Are you answer'd?

BASSANIO: This is no answer, thou unfeeling
man,
To excuse the current of thy cruelty.

SHYLOCK: I am not bound to please thee with
my answers.

BASSANIO: Do all men kill the things they do
not love?

SHYLOCK: Hates any man the thing he would
not kill?

BASSANIO: Every offence is not a hate at first.

SHYLOCK: What, wouldst thou have a serpent
sting thee twice?

ANTONIO: I pray you, think you question with
the Jew:
You may as well go stand upon the beach
And bid the main flood bate his usual height;
You may as well use question with the wolf
Why he hath made the ewe bleat for the lamb;
You may as well forbid the mountain pines
To wag their high tops and to make no noise,

When they are fretten with the gusts of heaven;

You may as well do anything most hard,

As seek to soften that–than which what's harder?

His Jewish heart: therefore, I do beseech you,

Make no more offers, use no farther means,

But with all brief and plain conveniency

Let me have judgment and the Jew his will.

BASSANIO: For thy three thousand ducats here is six.

SHYLOCK: What judgment shall I dread, doing

Were in six parts and every part a ducat,

I would not draw them; I would have my bond.

DUKE: How shalt thou hope for mercy, rendering none?

SHYLOCK: What judgment shall I dread, doing no wrong?

You have among you many a purchased slave,

Which, like your asses and your dogs and mules,

You use in abject and in slavish parts,

Because you bought them: shall I say to you,

Let them be free, marry them to your heirs?

Why sweat they under burdens? let their beds

Be made as soft as yours and let their palates

Be season'd with such viands? You will answer

'The slaves are ours:' so do I answer you:

The pound of flesh, which I demand of him,

Is dearly bought; 'tis mine and I will have it.

If you deny me, fie upon your law!

There is no force in the decrees of Venice.

I stand for judgment: answer; shall I have it?

DUKE: Upon my power I may dismiss this court,

Unless Bellario, a learned doctor,

Whom I have sent for to determine this,

Come here to-day.

SALERIO: My lord, here stays without

A messenger with letters from the doctor,

New come from Padua.

DUKE: Bring us the letter; call the messenger.

BASSANIO: Good cheer, Antonio! What, man,

courage yet!

The Jew shall have my flesh, blood, bones and

all,

Ere thou shalt lose for me one drop of blood.

ANTONIO: I am a tainted wether of the flock,

Meetest for death: the weakest kind of fruit

Drops earliest to the ground; and so let me

You cannot better be employ'd, Bassanio,

Than to live still and write mine epitaph.

[*Enter NERISSA, dressed like a lawyer's clerk*]

DUKE: Came you from Padua, from Bellario?

NERISSA: From both, my lord. Bellario greets your grace.

[*Presenting a letter*]

BASSANIO: Why dost thou whet thy knife so earnestly?

SHYLOCK: To cut the forfeiture from that bankrupt there.

GRATIANO: Not on thy sole, but on thy soul, harsh Jew,

Thou makest thy knife keen; but no metal can,

No, not the hangman's axe, bear half the keenness

Of thy sharp envy. Can no prayers pierce thee?

SHYLOCK: No, none that thou hast wit enough to make.

GRATIANO: O, be thou damn'd, inexecrable dog!

And for thy life let justice be accused.

Thou almost makest me waver in my faith

To hold opinion with Pythagoras,

That souls of animals infuse themselves

Into the trunks of men: thy currish spirit

Govern'd a wolf, who, hang'd for human slaughter,

Even from the gallows did his fell soul fleet,

And, whilst thou lay'st in thy unhallow'd dam,

Infused itself in thee; for thy desires

Are wolvish, bloody, starved and ravenous.

SHYLOCK: Till thou canst rail the seal from off my bond,

Thou but offend'st thy lungs to speak so loud:

Repair thy wit, good youth, or it will fall

To cureless ruin. I stand here for law.

DUKE: This letter from Bellario doth commend

A young and learned doctor to our court.

Where is he?

NERISSA: He attendeth here hard by,

To know your answer, whether you'll admit him.

DUKE: With all my heart. Some three or four of you

Go give him courteous conduct to this place.

Meantime the court shall hear Bellario's letter.

Clerk: [Reads] Your grace shall understand that at the receipt of your letter I am very sick: but in the instant that your messenger came, in loving visitation was with me a young doctor of Rome;

his name is Balthasar. I acquainted him with the cause in controversy between the Jew and Antonio the merchant: we turned o'er many books together: he is furnished with my opinion; which, bettered with his own learning, the greatness whereof I cannot enough commend, comes with him, at my importunity, to fill up your grace's request in my stead. I beseech you, let his lack of years be no impediment to let him lack a reverend estimation; for I never knew so young a body with so old a head. I leave him to your gracious acceptance, whose trial shall better publish his commendation.

DUKE: You hear the learn'd Bellario, what he writes:

And here, I take it, is the doctor come.

[*Enter PORTIA, dressed like a doctor of laws*]

Give me your hand. Come you from old Bellario?

PORTIA: I did, my lord.

DUKE: You are welcome: take your place.

Are you acquainted with the difference

That holds this present question in the court?

PORTIA: I am informed thoroughly of the cause.

Which is the merchant here, and which the Jew?

DUKE: Antonio and old Shylock, both stand forth.

PORTIA: Is your name Shylock?

SHYLOCK: Shylock is my name.

PORTIA: Of a strange nature is the suit you follow;

Yet in such rule that the Venetian law

Cannot impugn you as you do proceed.

You stand within his danger, do you not?

ANTONIO: Ay, so he says.

PORTIA: Do you confess the bond?

ANTONIO: I do.

PORTIA: Then must the Jew be merciful.

SHYLOCK: On what compulsion must I? tell me that.

PORTIA: The quality of mercy is not strain'd,

It droppeth as the gentle rain from heaven

Upon the place beneath: it is twice blest;

It blesseth him that gives and him that takes:

'Tis mightiest in the mightiest: it becomes

The throned monarch better than his crown;

His sceptre shows the force of temporal power,

The attribute to awe and majesty,

Wherein doth sit the dread and fear of kings;

But mercy is above this sceptred sway;

It is enthroned in the hearts of kings,

It is an attribute to God himself;

And earthly power doth then show likest God's

When mercy seasons justice. Therefore, Jew,

Though justice be thy plea, consider this,

That, in the course of justice, none of us

Should see salvation: we do pray for mercy;

And that same prayer doth teach us all to render

The deeds of mercy. I have spoke thus much

To mitigate the justice of thy plea;

Which if thou follow, this strict court of Venice

Must needs give sentence 'gainst the merchant

there.

SHYLOCK: My deeds upon my head! I crave the

law,

The penalty and forfeit of my bond.

PORTIA: Is he not able to discharge the money?

BASSANIO: Yes, here I tender it for him in the

court;

Yea, twice the sum: if that will not suffice,

I will be bound to pay it ten times o'er,

On forfeit of my hands, my head, my heart:

If this will not suffice, it must appear

That malice bears down truth. And I beseech you,

Wrest once the law to your authority:

To do a great right, do a little wrong,

And curb this cruel devil of his will.

PORTIA: It must not be; there is no power in Venice

Can alter a decree established:

'Twill be recorded for a precedent,

And many an error by the same example

Will rush into the state: it cannot be.

SHYLOCK: A Daniel come to judgment! yea, a Daniel!

O wise young judge, how I do honour thee!

PORTIA: I pray you, let me look upon the bond.

SHYLOCK: Here 'tis, most reverend doctor, here it is.

PORTIA: Shylock, there's thrice thy money offer'd thee.

SHYLOCK: An oath, an oath, I have an oath in heaven:

Shall I lay perjury upon my soul?

No, not for Venice.

PORTIA: Why, this bond is forfeit;

And lawfully by this the Jew may claim
A pound of flesh, to be by him cut off
Nearest the merchant's heart. Be merciful:
Take thrice thy money; bid me tear the bond.

SHYLOCK: When it is paid according to the
tenor.
It doth appear you are a worthy judge;
You know the law, your exposition
Hath been most sound: I charge you by the law,
Whereof you are a well-deserving pillar,
Proceed to judgment: by my soul I swear
There is no power in the tongue of man
To alter me: I stay here on my bond.

ANTONIO: Most heartily I do beseech the court
To give the judgment.

PORTIA: Why then, thus it is:
You must prepare your bosom for his knife.

SHYLOCK: O noble judge! O excellent young
man!

PORTIA: For the intent and purpose of the law
Hath full relation to the penalty,
Which here appeareth due upon the bond.

SHYLOCK: 'Tis very true: O wise and upright
judge!

How much more elder art thou than thy looks!

PORTIA: Therefore lay bare your bosom.

SHYLOCK: Ay, his breast:

So says the bond: doth it not, noble judge?

'Nearest his heart:' those are the very words.

PORTIA: It is so. Are there balance here to weigh

The flesh?

SHYLOCK: I have them ready.

PORTIA: Have by some surgeon, Shylock, on your charge,

To stop his wounds, lest he do bleed to death.

SHYLOCK: Is it so nominated in the bond?

PORTIA: It is not so express'd: but what of that?

'Twere good you do so much for charity.

SHYLOCK: I cannot find it; 'tis not in the bond.

PORTIA: You, merchant, have you any thing to say?

ANTONIO: But little: I am arm'd and well prepared.

Give me your hand, Bassanio: fare you well!

Grieve not that I am fallen to this for you;

For herein Fortune shows herself more kind

Than is her custom: it is still her use

To let the wretched man outlive his wealth,

To view with hollow eye and wrinkled brow

An age of poverty; from which lingering penance

Of such misery doth she cut me off.

Commend me to your honourable wife:

Tell her the process of Antonio's end;

Say how I loved you, speak me fair in death;

And, when the tale is told, bid her be judge

Whether Bassanio had not once a love.

Repent but you that you shall lose your friend,

And he repents not that he pays your debt;

For if the Jew do cut but deep enough,

I'll pay it presently with all my heart.

BASSANIO: Antonio, I am married to a wife

Which is as dear to me as life itself;

But life itself, my wife, and all the world,

Are not with me esteem'd above thy life:

I would lose all, ay, sacrifice them all

Here to this devil, to deliver you.

PORTIA: Your wife would give you little thanks
for that,

If she were by, to hear you make the offer.

GRATIANO: I have a wife, whom, I protest, I
love:

I would she were in heaven, so she could

Entreat some power to change this currish Jew.

NERISSA: 'Tis well you offer it behind her back;

The wish would make else an unquiet house.

SHYLOCK: These be the Christian husbands. I have a daughter;

Would any of the stock of Barrabas

Had been her husband rather than a Christian!

[*Aside*]

We trifle time: I pray thee, pursue sentence.

PORTIA: A pound of that same merchant's flesh is thine:

The court awards it, and the law doth give it.

SHYLOCK: Most rightful judge!

PORTIA: And you must cut this flesh from off his breast:

The law allows it, and the court awards it.

SHYLOCK: Most learned judge! A sentence! Come, prepare!

PORTIA: Tarry a little; there is something else.

This bond doth give thee here no jot of blood;

The words expressly are 'a pound of flesh:'

Take then thy bond, take thou thy pound of flesh;

But, in the cutting it, if thou dost shed

One drop of Christian blood, thy lands and goods

Are, by the laws of Venice, confiscate

Unto the state of Venice.

GRATIANO: O upright judge! Mark, Jew: O

learned judge!

SHYLOCK: Is that the law?

PORTIA: Thyself shalt see the act:

For, as thou urgest justice, be assured

Thou shalt have justice, more than thou desirest.

GRATIANO: O learned judge! Mark, Jew: a

learned judge!

SHYLOCK: I take this offer, then; pay the bond

thrice

And let the Christian go.

BASSANIO: Here is the money.

PORTIA: Soft!

The Jew shall have all justice; soft! no haste:

He shall have nothing but the penalty.

GRATIANO: O Jew! an upright judge, a learned

judge!

PORTIA: Therefore prepare thee to cut off the

flesh.

Shed thou no blood, nor cut thou less nor more

But just a pound of flesh: if thou cut'st more

Or less than a just pound, be it but so much

As makes it light or heavy in the substance,

Or the division of the twentieth part

Of one poor scruple, nay, if the scale do turn

But in the estimation of a hair,

Thou diest and all thy goods are confiscate.

GRATIANO: A second Daniel, a Daniel, Jew!

Now, infidel, I have you on the hip.

PORTIA: Why doth the Jew pause? take thy
forfeiture.

SHYLOCK: Give me my principal, and let me go.

BASSANIO: I have it ready for thee; here it is.

PORTIA: He hath refused it in the open court:

He shall have merely justice and his bond.

GRATIANO: A Daniel, still say I, a second
Daniel!

I thank thee, Jew, for teaching me that word.

SHYLOCK: Shall I not have barely my principal?

PORTIA: Thou shalt have nothing but the
forfeiture,

To be so taken at thy peril, Jew.

SHYLOCK: Why, then the devil give him good of
it!

I'll stay no longer question.

PORTIA: Tarry, Jew:

The law hath yet another hold on you.

It is enacted in the laws of Venice,

If it be proved against an alien

That by direct or indirect attempts

He seek the life of any citizen,

The party 'gainst the which he doth contrive

Shall seize one half his goods; the other half

Comes to the privy coffer of the state;

And the offender's life lies in the mercy

Of the duke only, 'gainst all other voice.

In which predicament, I say, thou stand'st;

For it appears, by manifest proceeding,

That indirectly and directly too

Thou hast contrived against the very life

Of the defendant; and thou hast incurr'd

The danger formerly by me rehearsed.

Down therefore and beg mercy of the duke.

GRATIANO: Beg that thou mayst have leave to

hang thyself:

And yet, thy wealth being forfeit to the state,

Thou hast not left the value of a cord;

Therefore thou must be hang'd at the state's

charge.

DUKE: That thou shalt see the difference of our spirits,

I pardon thee thy life before thou ask it:

For half thy wealth, it is Antonio's;

The other half comes to the general state,

Which humbleness may drive unto a fine.

PORTIA: Ay, for the state, not for Antonio.

SHYLOCK: Nay, take my life and all; pardon not that:

You take my house when you do take the prop

That doth sustain my house; you take my life

When you do take the means whereby I live.

PORTIA: What mercy can you render him, Antonio?

GRATIANO: A halter gratis; nothing else, for God's sake.

ANTONIO: So please my lord the duke and all the court

To quit the fine for one half of his goods,

I am content; so he will let me have

The other half in use, to render it,

Upon his death, unto the gentleman

That lately stole his daughter:

Two things provided more, that, for this favour,

He presently become a Christian;

The other, that he do record a gift,

Here in the court, of all he dies possess'd,

Unto his son Lorenzo and his daughter.

DUKE: He shall do this, or else I do recant

The pardon that I late pronounced here.

PORTIA: Art thou contented, Jew? what dost

thou say?

SHYLOCK: I am content.

PORTIA: Clerk, draw a deed of gift.

SHYLOCK: I pray you, give me leave to go from

hence;

I am not well: send the deed after me,

And I will sign it.

DUKE: Get thee gone, but do it.

GRATIANO: In christening shalt thou have two

god-fathers:

Had I been judge, thou shouldst have had ten

more,

To bring thee to the gallows, not the font.

[*Exit SHYLOCK*]

DUKE: Sir, I entreat you home with me to dinner.

PORTIA: I humbly do desire your grace of

pardon:

I must away this night toward Padua,

And it is meet I presently set forth.

DUKE: I am sorry that your leisure serves you not.

Antonio, gratify this gentleman,

For, in my mind, you are much bound to him.

[*Exeunt Duke and his train*]

BASSANIO: Most worthy gentleman, I and my friend

Have by your wisdom been this day acquitted

Of grievous penalties; in lieu whereof,

Three thousand ducats, due unto the Jew,

We freely cope your courteous pains withal.

ANTONIO: And stand indebted, over and above,

In love and service to you evermore.

PORTIA: He is well paid that is well satisfied;

And I, delivering you, am satisfied

And therein do account myself well paid:

My mind was never yet more mercenary.

I pray you, know me when we meet again:

I wish you well, and so I take my leave.

BASSANIO: Dear sir, of force I must attempt you further:

Take some remembrance of us, as a tribute,

Not as a fee: grant me two things, I pray you,
Not to deny me, and to pardon me.

PORTIA: You press me far, and therefore I will
yield.

[*To ANTONIO*]

Give me your gloves, I'll wear them for your
sake;

[*To BASSANIO*]

And, for your love, I'll take this ring from you:
Do not draw back your hand; I'll take no more;
And you in love shall not deny me this.

BASSANIO: This ring, good sir, alas, it is a trifle!
I will not shame myself to give you this.

PORTIA: I will have nothing else but only this;
And now methinks I have a mind to it.

BASSANIO: There's more depends on this than
on the value.

The dearest ring in Venice will I give you,
And find it out by proclamation:
Only for this, I pray you, pardon me.

PORTIA: I see, sir, you are liberal in offers
You taught me first to beg; and now methinks
You teach me how a beggar should be answer'd.

BASSANIO: Good sir, this ring was given me by

my wife;

And when she put it on, she made me vow

That I should neither sell nor give nor lose it.

PORTIA: That 'scuse serves many men to save their gifts.

An if your wife be not a mad-woman,

And know how well I have deserved the ring,

She would not hold out enemy for ever,

For giving it to me. Well, peace be with you!

[*Exeunt Portia and Nerissa*]

ANTONIO: My Lord Bassanio, let him have the ring:

Let his deservings and my love withal

Be valued against your wife's commandment.

BASSANIO: Go, Gratiano, run and overtake him;

Give him the ring, and bring him, if thou canst,

Unto Antonio's house: away! make haste.

[*Exit Gratiano*]

Come, you and I will thither presently;

And in the morning early will we both

Fly toward Belmont: come, Antonio.

[*Exeunt*]

SCENE II. The same. A street.

[*Enter PORTIA and NERISSA*]

PORTIA: Inquire the Jew's house out, give him this deed

And let him sign it: we'll away to-night

And be a day before our husbands home:

This deed will be well welcome to Lorenzo.

[*Enter GRATIANO*]

GRATIANO: Fair sir, you are well o'erta'en

My Lord Bassanio upon more advice

Hath sent you here this ring, and doth entreat

Your company at dinner.

PORTIA: That cannot be:

His ring I do accept most thankfully:

And so, I pray you, tell him: furthermore,

I pray you, show my youth old Shylock's house.

GRATIANO: That will I do.

NERISSA: Sir, I would speak with you.

[*Aside to PORTIA*]

I'll see if I can get my husband's ring,

Which I did make him swear to keep for ever.

PORTIA: [Aside to NERISSA] Thou mayst, I warrant.

We shall have old swearing

That they did give the rings away to men;

But we'll outface them, and outswear them too.

[*Aloud*]

Away! make haste: thou knowist where I will

tarry.

NERISSA: Come, good sir, will you show me to

this house?

[*Exeunt*]

My Notes

ACT V

SCENE I. Belmont. The avenue to PORTIA'S house.

[*Enter LORENZO and JESSICA*]

LORENZO: The moon shines bright: in such a night as this,

When the sweet wind did gently kiss the trees

And they did make no noise, in such a night

Troilus methinks mounted the Troyan walls

And sigh'd his soul toward the Grecian tents,

Where Cressid lay that night.

JESSICA: In such a night

Did Thisbe fearfully o'ertrip the dew

And saw the lion's shadow ere himself

And ran dismay'd away.

LORENZO: In such a night

Stood Dido with a willow in her hand

Upon the wild sea banks and waft her love

To come again to Carthage.

JESSICA: In such a night

Medea gather'd the enchanted herbs

That did renew old AEson.

LORENZO: In such a night

Did Jessica steal from the wealthy Jew

And with an unthrift love did run from Venice

As far as Belmont.

JESSICA: In such a night

Did young Lorenzo swear he loved her well,

Stealing her soul with many vows of faith

And ne'er a true one.

LORENZO: In such a night

Did pretty Jessica, like a little shrew,

Slander her love, and he forgave it her.

JESSICA: I would out-night you, did no body come;

But, hark, I hear the footing of a man.

[*Enter STEPHANO*]

LORENZO: Who comes so fast in silence of the night?

STEPHANO: A friend.

LORENZO: A friend! what friend? your name, I pray you, friend?

STEPHANO: Stephano is my name; and I bring word

My mistress will before the break of day

Be here at Belmont; she doth stray about

By holy crosses, where she kneels and prays

For happy wedlock hours.

LORENZO: Who comes with her?

STEPHANO: None but a holy hermit and her

maid.

I pray you, is my master yet return'd?

LORENZO: He is not, nor we have not heard

from him.

But go we in, I pray thee, Jessica,

And ceremoniously let us prepare

Some welcome for the mistress of the house.

[*Enter LAUNCELOT*]

LAUNCELOT: Sola, sola! wo ha, ho! sola, sola!

LORENZO: Who calls?

LAUNCELOT: Sola! did you see Master

Lorenzo?

Master Lorenzo, sola, sola!

LORENZO: Leave hollaing, man: here.

LAUNCELOT: Sola! where? where?

LORENZO: Here.

LAUNCELOT: Tell him there's a post come from

my master, with his horn full of good news: my

master will be here ere morning.

[*Exit*]

LORENZO: Sweet soul, let's in, and there expect their coming.

And yet no matter: why should we go in?

My friend Stephano, signify, I pray you,

Within the house, your mistress is at hand;

And bring your music forth into the air.

[*Exit Stephano*]

How sweet the moonlight sleeps upon this bank!

Here will we sit and let the sounds of music

Creep in our ears: soft stillness and the night

Become the touches of sweet harmony.

Sit, Jessica. Look how the floor of heaven

Is thick inlaid with patines of bright gold:

There's not the smallest orb which thou behold'st

But in his motion like an angel sings,

Still quiring to the young-eyed cherubins;

Such harmony is in immortal souls;

But whilst this muddy vesture of decay

Doth grossly close it in, we cannot hear it.

[*Enter Musicians*]

Come, ho! and wake Diana with a hymn!

With sweetest touches pierce your mistress' ear,

And draw her home with music.

[*Music*]

JESSICA: I am never merry when I hear sweet music.

LORENZO: The reason is, your spirits are attentive:
For do but note a wild and wanton herd,
Or race of youthful and unhandled colts,
Fetching mad bounds, bellowing and neighing loud,
Which is the hot condition of their blood;
If they but hear perchance a trumpet sound,
Or any air of music touch their ears,
You shall perceive them make a mutual stand,
Their savage eyes turn'd to a modest gaze
By the sweet power of music: therefore the poet
Did feign that Orpheus drew trees, stones and floods;
Since nought so stockish, hard and full of rage,
But music for the time doth change his nature.
The man that hath no music in himself,
Nor is not moved with concord of sweet sounds,
Is fit for treasons, stratagems and spoils;
The motions of his spirit are dull as night
And his affections dark as Erebus:
Let no such man be trusted. Mark the music.

[*Enter PORTIA and NERISSA*]

PORTIA: That light we see is burning in my hall.

How far that little candle throws his beams!

So shines a good deed in a naughty world.

NERISSA: When the moon shone, we did not

see the candle.

PORTIA: So doth the greater glory dim the less:

A substitute shines brightly as a king

Unto the king be by, and then his state

Empties itself, as doth an inland brook

Into the main of waters. Music! hark!

NERISSA: It is your music, madam, of the

house.

PORTIA: Nothing is good, I see, without respect:

Methinks it sounds much sweeter than by day.

NERISSA: Silence bestows that virtue on it,

madam.

PORTIA: The crow doth sing as sweetly as the

lark,

When neither is attended, and I think

The nightingale, if she should sing by day,

When every goose is cackling, would be thought

No better a musician than the wren.

How many things by season season'd are

To their right praise and true perfection!

Peace, ho! the moon sleeps with Endymion

And would not be awaked.

[*Music ceases*]

LORENZO: That is the voice,

Or I am much deceived, of Portia.

PORTIA: He knows me as the blind man knows

the cuckoo,

By the bad voice.

LORENZO: Dear lady, welcome home.

PORTIA: We have been praying for our

husbands' healths,

Which speed, we hope, the better for our words.

Are they return'd?

LORENZO: Madam, they are not yet;

But there is come a messenger before,

To signify their coming.

PORTIA: Go in, Nerissa;

Give order to my servants that they take

No note at all of our being absent hence;

Nor you, Lorenzo; Jessica, nor you.

[*A tucket sounds*]

LORENZO: Your husband is at hand; I hear his

trumpet:

We are no tell-tales, madam; fear you not.

PORTIA: This night methinks is but the daylight sick;

It looks a little paler: 'tis a day,

Such as the day is when the sun is hid.

[*Enter BASSANIO, ANTONIO, GRATIANO, and their followers*]

BASSANIO: We should hold day with the Antipodes,

If you would walk in absence of the sun.

PORTIA: Let me give light, but let me not be light;

For a light wife doth make a heavy husband,

And never be Bassanio so for me:

But God sort all! You are welcome home, my lord.

BASSANIO: I thank you, madam. Give welcome to my friend.

This is the man, this is Antonio,

To whom I am so infinitely bound.

PORTIA: You should in all sense be much bound to him.

For, as I hear, he was much bound for you.

ANTONIO: No more than I am well acquitted of.

PORTIA: Sir, you are very welcome to our
house:
It must appear in other ways than words,
Therefore I scant this breathing courtesy.
GRATIANO: [To NERISSA] By yonder moon I
swear you do me wrong;
In faith, I gave it to the judge's clerk:
Would he were gelt that had it, for my part,
Since you do take it, love, so much at heart.
PORTIA: A quarrel, ho, already! what's the
matter?
GRATIANO: About a hoop of gold, a paltry ring
That she did give me, whose posy was
For all the world like cutler's poetry
Upon a knife, 'Love me, and leave me not.'
NERISSA: What talk you of the posy or the
value?
You swore to me, when I did give it you,
That you would wear it till your hour of death
And that it should lie with you in your grave:
Though not for me, yet for your vehement oaths,
You should have been respective and have kept
it.
Gave it a judge's clerk! no, God's my judge,

The clerk will ne'er wear hair on's face that had it.

GRATIANO: He will, an if he live to be a man.

NERISSA: Ay, if a woman live to be a man.

GRATIANO: Now, by this hand, I gave it to a youth,
A kind of boy, a little scrubbed boy,
No higher than thyself; the judge's clerk,
A prating boy, that begg'd it as a fee:
I could not for my heart deny it him.

PORTIA: You were to blame, I must be plain with you,
To part so slightly with your wife's first gift:
A thing stuck on with oaths upon your finger
And so riveted with faith unto your flesh.
I gave my love a ring and made him swear
Never to part with it; and here he stands;
I dare be sworn for him he would not leave it
Nor pluck it from his finger, for the wealth
That the world masters. Now, in faith, Gratiano,
You give your wife too unkind a cause of grief:
An 'twere to me, I should be mad at it.

BASSANIO: [Aside] Why, I were best to cut my left hand off

And swear I lost the ring defending it.

GRATIANO: My Lord Bassanio gave his ring away

Unto the judge that begg'd it and indeed

Deserved it too; and then the boy, his clerk,

That took some pains in writing, he begg'd mine;

And neither man nor master would take aught

But the two rings.

PORTIA: What ring gave you my lord?

Not that, I hope, which you received of me.

BASSANIO: If I could add a lie unto a fault,

I would deny it; but you see my finger

Hath not the ring upon it; it is gone.

PORTIA: Even so void is your false heart of truth.

By heaven, I will ne'er come in your bed

Until I see the ring.

NERISSA: Nor I in yours

Till I again see mine.

BASSANIO: Sweet Portia,

If you did know to whom I gave the ring,

If you did know for whom I gave the ring

And would conceive for what I gave the ring

And how unwillingly I left the ring,

When nought would be accepted but the ring,
You would abate the strength of your
displeasure.

PORTIA: If you had known the virtue of the ring,
Or half her worthiness that gave the ring,
Or your own honour to contain the ring,
You would not then have parted with the ring.
What man is there so much unreasonable,
If you had pleased to have defended it
With any terms of zeal, wanted the modesty
To urge the thing held as a ceremony?
Nerissa teaches me what to believe:
I'll die for't but some woman had the ring.

BASSANIO: No, by my honour, madam, by my
soul,
No woman had it, but a civil doctor,
Which did refuse three thousand ducats of me
And begg'd the ring; the which I did deny him
And suffer'd him to go displeased away;
Even he that did uphold the very life
Of my dear friend. What should I say, sweet
lady?
I was enforced to send it after him;
I was beset with shame and courtesy;

My honour would not let ingratitude

So much besmear it. Pardon me, good lady;

For, by these blessed candles of the night,

Had you been there, I think you would have begg'd

The ring of me to give the worthy doctor.

PORTIA: Let not that doctor e'er come near my house:

Since he hath got the jewel that I loved,

And that which you did swear to keep for me,

I will become as liberal as you;

I'll not deny him any thing I have,

No, not my body nor my husband's bed:

Know him I shall, I am well sure of it:

Lie not a night from home; watch me like Argus:

If you do not, if I be left alone,

Now, by mine honour, which is yet mine own,

I'll have that doctor for my bedfellow.

NERISSA: And I his clerk; therefore be well advised

How you do leave me to mine own protection.

GRATIANO: Well, do you so; let not me take him, then;

For if I do, I'll mar the young clerk's pen.

ANTONIO: I am the unhappy subject of these quarrels.

PORTIA: Sir, grieve not you; you are welcome notwithstanding.

BASSANIO: Portia, forgive me this enforced wrong;

And, in the hearing of these many friends,

I swear to thee, even by thine own fair eyes,

Wherein I see myself–

PORTIA: Mark you but that!

In both my eyes he doubly sees himself;

In each eye, one: swear by your double self,

And there's an oath of credit.

BASSANIO: Nay, but hear me:

Pardon this fault, and by my soul I swear

I never more will break an oath with thee.

ANTONIO: I once did lend my body for his wealth;

Which, but for him that had your husband's ring,

Had quite miscarried: I dare be bound again,

My soul upon the forfeit, that your lord

Will never more break faith advisedly.

PORTIA: Then you shall be his surety. Give him this

And bid him keep it better than the other.

ANTONIO: Here, Lord Bassanio; swear to keep this ring.

BASSANIO: By heaven, it is the same I gave the doctor!

PORTIA: I had it of him: pardon me, Bassanio;
For, by this ring, the doctor lay with me.

NERISSA: And pardon me, my gentle Gratiano;
For that same scrubbed boy, the doctor's clerk,
In lieu of this last night did lie with me.

GRATIANO: Why, this is like the mending of highways
In summer, where the ways are fair enough:
What, are we cuckolds ere we have deserved it?

PORTIA: Speak not so grossly. You are all amazed:
Here is a letter; read it at your leisure;
It comes from Padua, from Bellario:
There you shall find that Portia was the doctor,
Nerissa there her clerk: Lorenzo here
Shall witness I set forth as soon as you
And even but now return'd; I have not yet
Enter'd my house. Antonio, you are welcome;
And I have better news in store for you

Than you expect: unseal this letter soon;

There you shall find three of your argosies

Are richly come to harbour suddenly:

You shall not know by what strange accident

I chanced on this letter.

ANTONIO: I am dumb.

BASSANIO: Were you the doctor and I knew
you not?

GRATIANO: Were you the clerk that is to make
me cuckold?

NERISSA: Ay, but the clerk that never means to
do it,

Unless he live until he be a man.

BASSANIO: Sweet doctor, you shall be my bedfellow:

When I am absent, then lie with my wife.

ANTONIO: Sweet lady, you have given me life
and living;

For here I read for certain that my ships

Are safely come to road.

PORTIA: How now, Lorenzo!

My clerk hath some good comforts too for you.

NERISSA: Ay, and I'll give them him without a
fee.

There do I give to you and Jessica,

From the rich Jew, a special deed of gift,

After his death, of all he dies possess'd of.

LORENZO: Fair ladies, you drop manna in the

way

Of starved people.

PORTIA: It is almost morning,

And yet I am sure you are not satisfied

Of these events at full. Let us go in;

And charge us there upon inter'gatories,

And we will answer all things faithfully.

GRATIANO: Let it be so: the first inter'gatory

That my Nerissa shall be sworn on is,

Whether till the next night she had rather stay,

Or go to bed now, being two hours to day:

But were the day come, I should wish it dark,

That I were couching with the doctor's clerk.

Well, while I live I'll fear no other thing

So sore as keeping safe Nerissa's ring.

[*Exeunt*]

My Notes

Glossary of Literary Terms

Alliteration: The occurrence of identical sounds, most often at the beginning of words e.g. "From forth the fatal loins of these two foes"

Allusion: An indirect reference to something

Anaphora: Repetition of the same word or phrase at the beginning of consecutive lines

Antagonist: The **protagonist**'s main adversary.

Antithesis: A person or thing that is the opposite of something else

Aside: A character's remark that is only meant to be heard by the audience but unheard by other characters in the play

Assonance: The resemblance of sounds between vowels of words in close proximity to one another

Blank verse: **Poetry** written with a regular **metre** but unrhymed, almost always in **iambic pentameter**

Climax: The dramatic end to the main **plot**. This is usually followed by **falling action**

Couplet: Two successive rhyming lines

Dramatic monologue: A poem in the form of a speech of an individual character

Euphemism: A gentle way of expressing something unpleasant

Falling Action: The section of a story following the **climax** but before the very end of the story

Foil: A character providing a contrast with another

Foot: A combination of stressed and unstressed syllables

Heroic couplet: a pair of rhyming **iambic pentameters**

Hyperbole: Exaggerated statements not meant to be taken literally

Iambic pentameter: A line of verse with five metrical feet, each consisting of one unstressed syllable followed by one stressed syllable

Imagery: A visually descriptive use of language

Internal rhyme: A rhyme involving a word in the middle of a line

Metaphor: A figure of speech that applies words to describe something in a non-literal way (e.g. *coal black eyes*). Metaphors do not use the words "like" or "as". If these words are used it is a **simile** (e.g. *eyes as black as coal*, or *eyes like black coal*).

Metre: The basic rhythmic structure of a verse or lines in a verse

Motif: An image or idea that runs through a play or novel

Onomatopoeia: A word that resembles the sound it is describing e.g. cuckoo, woof, burp, etc

Oxymoron: A figure of speech containing contradictory words, e.g. deafening silence

Paradox: A statement that contradicts itself e.g "This sentence is not true"

Personification: Attributing human characteristics to inanimate things

Plot: The events that make up the main part of a story

Poetry: Rhymed or rhythmic text

Pronoun: Referring to a person or thing, e.g. I, you, she, this, that

Prose: Written or spoken language without rhyme or rhythm

Protagonist: The lead character

Quatrain: A **stanza** of four lines

Refrain: A word or series of words repeated at intervals within a poem

Simile: A figure of speech containing "as" or "like" to describe something in a non-literal way (e.g. eyes like black coal). If the words "like" or "as" are not used then it is a **metaphor** (e.g. coal black eyes).

Soliloquy: A speech spoken by a character when alone, revealing their innermost thoughts

Sonnet: A fourteen-line poem.

Stanza: A group of poetic lines resembling paragraphs in **prose**

Sub-plot: A plot separate to the main **plot**

Syntax: The arrangement of words and phrases within a sentence

Tragic Hero: Generally the **protagonist** whose flaws or mistakes lead to their downfall

Glossary

Amity – Friendship

Argosy – Merchant Ships

Barrabas – Man chosen by crowd over Jesus to be set free by Pontius Pilate

Cozen – Lying or cheating

Divers – Various or many

Doublet – A type of jacket

Drudge – Lowly servant who carries out menial work

Ducat – A gold coin

Ergo – Therefore

Fretten – Rubbed

Gratis – Free

Impertinent – Rude

Janus – Two-headed roman God

Knave – deceitful person

Knell – the solemn ring of a bell, usually for a death or funeral

Lineament – Ointment to relieve pain

Mars – God of war

Obdurate – Stubborn

Phoebus – Greek god, also known as Apollo

Presage – Foreshadow

Pythagoras – Greek mathematician

Rail – Rage against something

Sepulchre – Grave

Surfeit – Excess

Unhallow'd – Unholy

For more on our large print, dyslexia-friendly, and annotation-friendly books, as well as our bulk discounts for schools visit:

firestonebooks.com

Printed in Great Britain
by Amazon